The Walter Lynwood Fleming Lectures in Southern History
Louisiana State University

WHAT THEY FOUGHT FOR

1861 — 1865

WHAT THEY FOUGHT FOR 1861 – 1865

JAMES M. McPHERSON

ANCHOR BOOKS
DOUBLEDAY
New York   London   Toronto   Sydney   Auckland

AN ANCHOR BOOK

PUBLISHED BY DOUBLEDAY

a division of Bantam Doubleday Dell Publishing Group, Inc.
1540 Broadway, New York, New York 10036

ANCHOR BOOKS, DOUBLEDAY, and the portrayal of an anchor are
trademarks of Doubleday, a division of Bantam Doubleday Dell
Publishing Group, Inc.

What They Fought For, 1861–1865 was originally published in
hardcover by Louisiana State University Press in 1994. The
Anchor Books edition is published by arrangement with Louisiana
State University Press.

Designer: Amanda McDonald Key

Library of Congress Cataloging-in-Publication Data

McPherson, James M.
     What they fought for, 1861–1865 / James M. McPherson—
1st Anchor Books ed.
          p.   cm.
     Originally published: Baton Rouge : Louisiana State
University Press, c1994, in series: The Walter Lynwood Fleming
lectures in southern history.
     Includes bibliographical references (p.   ) and index.
     1. United States—History—Civil War, 1861–1865—Causes.
I. Title.
E459.M24   1995
973.7′11—dc20   94-38423
                                                          CIP

ISBN 0-385-47634-5
Copyright © 1994 by Louisiana State University Press

All Rights Reserved
Printed in the United States of America
First Anchor Books edition: April 1995

10 9 8 7 6 5 4 3 2 1

For Patricia, a helpmeet in more ways than one

Contents

PREFACE

During the whole of my professional life I have been aware of the Walter Lynwood Fleming Lectures as the most important lecture series in the field of southern history. Much significant new work on slavery, sectional conflict, the Confederacy, Reconstruction, race relations, and a host of other topics has received its initial exposure in these lectures. The leading scholars of southern history in the past half century have served as Fleming lecturers. My own mentor, C. Vann Woodward, has done so twice.

I was most pleased and flattered, therefore, to be invited to deliver the fifty-fifth series of Fleming Lectures in 1993. My experiences during those beautiful spring days at Louisiana State University were all I could have hoped for, and more. The Department of History proved to be a wonderful host. The audiences for the three lectures were most stimulating, and the questions they asked have helped to clarify my thinking in the best tradition of intellectual discourse. I wish to thank Professor William J. Cooper and Professor Paul F. Paskoff, acting chairman of the Department of History, for making my stay on the LSU campus so pleasant. Bill Cooper and his wife, Patricia, were generous hosts not only on this occasion but also on a previous visit to the Hill Memorial Library at LSU, where I did part of the research for these lectures.

In preparing the lectures for publication I have received

the efficient assistance of the staff of the LSU Press. I appreciate the opportunity they have provided to make my findings available to a wider audience. The lectures appear here in a form only slightly altered from their oral delivery, in the hope that the direct, rather than discursive, style required by the lecture format will retain its effectiveness on the printed page.

Historical research is impossible without the help of librarians and curators of manuscript collections. The personnel of the seventeen libraries and historical societies where I did research for this book are too numerous to name individually. But I must single out for particular mention the staffs of the Huntington Library in San Marino, California, which possesses not only a superb collection of Civil War books but also nearly fifty manuscript collections of soldiers' letters or diaries and of the Southern Historical Collection at the University of North Carolina and the Perkins Library at Duke University, which have the two largest collections of Confederate soldiers' letters and diaries, as well as many Union collections. I owe a special debt of gratitude to Dr. Richard Sommers, archivist of the United States Army Military History Institute at Carlisle, Pennsylvania, who guided me through the rich and multitudinous collections of letters and diaries, especially of Union soldiers, in that repository. And I must also thank Peter Michel and his staff at the Missouri Historical Society in St. Louis, who graciously gave me access to their collections during a distracting move into a new building.

Several individuals have allowed me access to copies of soldiers' letters in private possession; for this generosity and kindness I wish to thank O. Vernon Burton, J. M. Dobie, Dave Holmquist, Pat Knobloch, Henry Perry, and Hal Saffell.

Research for this project began at the Huntington Library in 1987. My thanks go to Martin Ridge, then the director of research at the Huntington, and to the Seaver Institute, which funded my year at the Huntington, for their support and encouragement. Princeton University and its University Committee on Research in the Humanities and Social Sciences have generously granted me two leaves from teaching duties and financial support for research on this and related projects.

Finally, and most important, I wish to express love and gratitude to my wife, Patricia, who has read almost as many soldiers' letters and diaries as I have. She is a superb research assistant, which is only one of the many virtues that have enriched my life during our thirty-six years of marriage. The dedication expresses only a small measure of my debt to her.

Abbreviations

CWTI Collection, USAMHI: *Civil War Times Illustrated Collection, United States Army Military History Institute, Carlisle, Pennsylvania*

HEH: *Henry E. Huntington Library, San Marino, California*

HML, LSU: *Hill Memorial Library, Louisiana State University, Baton Rouge*

HRT Collection, USAMHI: *Harrisburg Civil War Round Table Collection, United States Army Military History Institute, Carlisle, Pennsylvania*

ISHL: *Illinois State Historical Library, Springfield*

MDHS: *Maryland Historical Society, Baltimore*

MNHS: *Minnesota Historical Society, St. Paul*

OHS: *Ohio Historical Society, Columbus*

PLDU: *Perkins Library, Duke University, Durham, North Carolina*

SHC, UNC: *Southern Historical Collection, University of North Carolina, Chapel Hill*

TSL: *Tennessee State Library, Nashville*

USAMHI: *United States Army Military History Institute, Carlisle, Pennsylvania*

VHS: *Virginia Historical Society, Richmond*

WHAT THEY FOUGHT FOR

1861 — 1865

INTRODUCTION

The subject of this small book is carved from research for a larger book tentatively entitled *Why They Fought*. That book will explore the motives of Union and Confederate soldiers for enlisting and fighting in the Civil War. The principal sources for that book, and this one, are the personal letters and diaries written by soldiers during their war experience. These are sources of unparalleled richness and candor— richness because Civil War armies were the most literate in all history to that time and the letters of their soldiers have been preserved in matchless abundance for historians to read; candor because unlike modern armies, those of the Civil War did not discourage diary keeping or subject soldiers' letters to censorship. Thus we can get closer to the real thoughts and emotions of Civil War soldiers than to those of any other war.

In *Why They Fought* I expect to focus on a range of attitudes and motives among these mostly volunteer soldiers, including peer pressure; group cohesion; male bonding; ideals of manhood and masculinity; concepts of duty, honor, and courage; functions of leadership, discipline, and coercion; and the role of religion as well as of the darker passions of hatred and vengeance. I intend to discuss how these young men coped with fear, stress, exhaustion, pain, and death. A final theme that will receive attention is ideology—that is, what Civil War soldiers believed they were fighting for. This theme has emerged to greater importance than I expected when I began the project. Indeed, it is of sufficient importance to merit full-scale treatment on its own. I therefore chose it as the subject for the Walter Lynwood Fleming Lectures that have become this book.

There exists, however, a general impression that Civil War soldiers had little or no idea of what they were fighting for, and therefore that the subject of the book is a nonsubject. In William Faulkner's novel *Sartoris,* someone asks a Confederate veteran what that war had been about. He replies, "Damned if I ever did know." A study of Tennessee soldiers based on questionnaires completed in the early 1920s by surviving veterans concluded that "few Tennesseans were conscious of the major issues of the Civil War, and fewer still had any concept of the South's goals." In 1992 the commander of the New York chapter of the Sons of Union Veterans said that "it wasn't because our fathers knew what they were fighting for that they were heroes. They didn't know what they were fighting for, exactly, and they fought on anyway. That's what made them heroes." [1]

Two recent studies of the psychology and world view of Civil War soldiers, Gerald Linderman's *Embattled Courage* and Reid Mitchell's *Civil War Soldiers,* present evidence of ideological awareness among these men. Nevertheless, Linderman maintains that "even 'The Cause' reduced itself to a manifestation of courage"—the theme of his book—and Mitchell states that "men may well have fought during the Civil War for reasons having less to do with ideology than with masculine identity." [2] The great pioneer in scholarly studies of Civil War soldiers, Bell Irvin Wiley, put it more bluntly: with respect to Confederate fighting men, he wrote that "it is doubtful whether many of them either understood or cared about the Constitutional issues at stake." As for Billy Yank, "One searches most letters and diaries in vain for soldiers' comment on why they were in the war or for what they were fighting. . . . American soldiers of the 1860s appear to have been about as little concerned with ideological issues as were those of the 1940s."[3]

The comparison is a reference to numerous studies of GIs in World War II, especially the four-volume work entitled *The American Soldier*. This exhaustive treatise by psychologists, sociologists, and military analysts established a paradigm that has governed research on combat motivation ever since. Simply put, the paradigm states that "primary group cohesion" is the main factor motivating soldiers in combat—that is, solidarity with one's comrades in squad or platoon or company, the bonding that enables men facing a common danger to fight as a unit in which the survival of each member of the group depends on the others' doing their jobs, and the survival and performance of the group depends on the steadiness of each individual. It is not "belief in a cause" that motivates men to fight, wrote Brigadier General S. L. A. Marshall in his classic statement of this thesis, *Men Against Fire,* published in 1947; when the chips are down, "a man fights to help the man next to him. . . . Men do not fight for a cause but because they do not want to let their comrades down."[4]

A corollary of this paradigm relegates patriotism and ideology to a negligible, almost nonexistent place in the combat soldier's world view. *The American Soldier* quoted one GI: "Ask any dogface on the line. You're fighting for your skin on the line. When I enlisted I was patriotic as all hell. There's no patriotism on the line. A boy up there 60 days on the line is in danger every minute. He ain't fighting for patriotism."[5] A British officer said that "it would be foolish to imagine that the average British or American soldier went into battle thinking he was helping to save democracy. . . . He never gave democracy a thought." In fact, among GIs there was "a taboo against any talk of a flag-waving variety."[6]

If this is true, and if Bell Wiley is right that Civil War soldiers were like those of World War II, and if the other statements quoted above are correct that Johnny Reb and Billy Yank had no idea what they were fighting for, the subject of this book is indeed a nonsubject. But my research has led me to a different conclusion. The ideological motifs that almost leaped from so many pages of the letters and diaries of Civil War soldiers have caused me to reject the paradigm as far as they were concerned. Not all, of course, but a large number of those men in blue and gray were intensely aware of the issues at stake and passionately concerned about them.

To set the stage for the evidence I will present to support this assertion, it is worth noting again that these were the most literate armies in history to that time—more than 80 percent of Confederate soldiers and more than 90 percent of white Union soldiers could read and write. Most of them were volunteers, in contrast to twentieth-century wars in which most soldiers have been draftees or long-service regulars. Those citizen-soldiers of the Civil War came from the world's most politicized and democratic society. Their median age at enlistment was twenty-four, which meant that a majority of them had voted in the election of 1860, the most heated and momentous election in American history. They continued to vote during the war, not only electing some of their company and regimental officers but also voting in state and national elections. Americans were the world's preeminent newspaper-reading people in the nineteenth century. Soldiers continued this habit during the war whenever possible, eagerly snapping up newspapers that were sometimes available in camp only a day or two after publication. Nor did the taboo against discussion of ideological issues that seemed to prevail in World War II exist during the Civil War.

Here are a few of many examples that could be cited to illustrate these points. A Mississippi private wrote in his diary during the winter of 1862: "Spend much time in reading daily papers & discussing the war question." Two years later an Alabama officer in the trenches at Petersburg wrote to his wife: "We have daily access to the Richmond papers. . . . We spend much of our time in reading these journals and discussing the situation."[7] During the months before the northern presidential election of 1864, an Ohio cavalry sergeant made the following entries in his diary. September 10: "Political news very exciting." September 12: "Politics the principal topic of the day." September 13: "Spent a good portion of my time reading the news and arguing politics." His regiment then went on a raid; after they returned he resumed such entries—for example, October 15: "Considerable excitement on politics in camp."[8]

Several units established debating societies during less active times in winter quarters. An Illinois sergeant's diary described one of these debates in his camp near Vicksburg during the winter of 1863–1864: "Took part on the affirmative of Resolved that the Constitutional relations of the rebel states should be fixed by Congress only." Another debate, he wrote, "discussed the question of reducing rebel states to territories. . . . Witnessed some rare outbursts of untutored eloquence." On yet another occasion, "Sergt. Miller expanded on the revolution of ideas" and the writer of the diary himself "expressed my views freely to my comrades upon policy and duty in this crisis."[9]

Some officers were not pleased with these disputatious activities. "A soldier [should have] naught to do with politics," wrote one Union colonel. "The nearer he approaches a machine . . . the more valuable he becomes to the service. Our soldiers are too intelligent, for they will talk and they will write, and read the papers." But this was distinctly a minority view. A New York captain wrote to his wife in 1864 that "our soldiers are closer thinkers and reasoners than the people at home. It is the soldiers who have educated the people . . . to a just perception of their duties in this contest." And none other than Ulysses S. Grant noted with pride after the war that "our armies were composed of men who were able to read, men who knew what they were fighting for." [10] The same could be said of Confederate soldiers.

What did those men in blue and gray believe they were fighting for? A sentence in that letter of the New York captain offers a clue: "Every soldier [knows] he [is] fighting not only for his own liberty but [even] more for the liberty of the human race for all time to come." Another clue is provided by a wounded Union private who described a debating society organized by convalescent soldiers during the last winter of the war. Among other questions, they debated the following: "Resolved that the present struggle will do more to establish and maintain a republican form of government than the Revolutionary war." [11]

These themes of liberty and republicanism formed the ideological core of the cause for which Civil War soldiers fought, Confederate as well as Union. Americans in both North and South believed themselves custodians of the legacy of 1776. The crisis of 1861 was the great test of whether they were worthy of the heritage of liberty bequeathed to them by the founding fathers. On *their* shoulders rode the fate of the great experiment in republican government launched in 1776. Both Abraham Lincoln and Jefferson Davis appealed to this intense consciousness of parallels between 1776 and 1861. That is why Lincoln began his great evocation of Union war aims with the words: "Four score and seven years ago our fathers brought forth on this continent, a new nation, conceived in Liberty." Likewise, Davis urged his people to "renew such sacrifices as our fathers made to the holy cause of constitutional liberty." [12]

The profound irony of the Civil War was that Confederate

and Union soldiers, like Davis and Lincoln, interpreted the heritage of 1776 in opposite ways. Confederates fought for liberty and independence from what they regarded as a tyrannical government; Unionists fought to preserve the nation created by the founders from dismemberment and destruction. Chapter 1 will explore Confederate elucidations of this and related themes; chapter 2 will look at the Union side; chapter 3 will analyze the perceptions of the slavery issue by both Confederate and Union soldiers.

1

"THE HOLY CAUSE OF LIBERTY AND INDEPENDENCE"

Invoking his state's Revolutionary motto, *Sic Semper Tyrannis,* a young Virginia officer filled letters to his mother with comparisons of the North's "war of subjugation against the South" to "England's war upon the colonies." He was confident that the Confederacy would win this "second War for American Independence" because "Tyranny cannot prosper in the nineteenth century" against "a people fighting for their liberties." An enlisted man in a Texas cavalry regiment told his sister in 1861 that just as their forefathers had rebelled against King George to establish "*Liberty* and freedom in this western world . . . so we dissolved our alliance with this oppressive foe and are now enlisted in 'The Holy Cause of Liberty and Independence' again."[1]

The great patriotic holidays especially called forth such sentiments in the letters and diaries of southern soldiers. On Washington's Birthday in 1862, a captain in the 5th Alabama Infantry wrote to his mother: "How trifling were the wrongs complained of by our Revolutionary forefathers, in comparison with ours! If the mere imposition of a tax could raise such a tumult what should be the result of the terrible system of oppression instituted by the Yankees?" On the Fourth of July the same year, a Kentuckian who had cast his lot with the Confederacy reflected in his diary on George Washington, "who set us an example in bursting the bonds of tyranny" to fight for "those inestimable and priceless rights . . . obtained by our forefathers and bequeathed to us." Exactly a year later, an Alabama corporal who had just been captured at Gettysburg nevertheless expressed confidence that, fighting for "the same principles which fired the hearts of our ancestors in the revolutionary struggle," the South would ultimately win the war.[2]

The memory of defeats followed by eventual victory in the Revolution helped bolster Confederate morale in similar times of trouble. During the retreat from Gettysburg, a Georgia captain in the Army of Northern Virginia learned of the surrender of Vicksburg. "What a calamity!" he wrote to his wife. "But let us not despair. . . . We must put forth even greater energy—resolve more fully to conquer or die. Our forefathers were whipped in nearly every battle & lost their capital & yet after seven years of trials and hardships achieved their independence." A farmer's son serving in the 1st North Carolina Infantry wrote to his father during another period of Confederate reverses: "Instead of indulging in feelings of despondency let us compare our situation and cause to those of our illustrious ancestors who achieved the liberties we have ever enjoyed and for which we are now contending."[3]

Whether or not they compared their own war for independence with the Revolution of 1776, the letters and diaries of many Confederate soldiers bristled with rhetoric of liberty and self-government and with expressions of a willingness to die for the cause. The writers of these letters ranged from the prominent to the obscure. They included the wealthy Alabama planter who married one of Mary Todd Lincoln's half sisters and who as a captain in the 4th Alabama declared that "I am willing to fall for the cause of Liberty and Independence," and the Georgia dirt farmer writing to his wife in 1864 from the trenches at Petersburg that "if I fall Let me fall for I will fall in a good cose for if I can not git Liberty I perfer death."[4] They also included the son of a rich Baltimore merchant who defied the wishes of his Unionist father and enlisted in the 44th Virginia. In a letter written three months before he was killed at Chancellorsville, this soldier explained to his father that he considered the war "a struggle between Liberty on one side, and Tyranny on the other." That is why "I determined to . . . espouse the holy cause of Southern freedom." A Louisiana corporal in the Army of Northern Virginia who also lost his life in the conflict had written a friend that this "struggle for liberty" was "a glorious & holy one and I for one am willing that my bones shall bleach the sacred soil of Virginia in driving the envading host of tyrants from our soil." A Missouri lieutenant who was wounded at Pea Ridge wrote in his diary while recovering from the wound that if he was killed, it would be while "fighting gloriously for the undying principles of Constitutional liberty and self government." Two years later he was killed in action near Atlanta.[5]

These voices of commitment to liberty and self-government shaded into simple but heartfelt avowals of patriotism. The Confederacy was their country; they felt a sense of duty to this country that had called on them to defend its very existence. "Sink or swim, survive or perish," wrote a young Kentuckian who went with the South, "I will fight in defence of my country." A lieutenant in the 47th Alabama, a farmer who owned a few slaves, wrote to his wife in 1862: "I confess that I gave you up with reluctance. Yet I love my country dearly. The war in which we are unfortunately involved has been forced upon us. We have asked for nothing but to be let alone. I intend to discharge my duty to my country and to my God." Like many others, he too made the supreme sacrifice to fulfill that duty, and never returned to see the wife and two children he missed so much.[6]

When prospects for the Confederacy appeared bright,

these convictions took the form of an expansive nationalism. A University of Georgia student who left school to enlist when the war broke out wrote to his sweetheart in 1862 that "we are living in the midst of the grandest revolution ever known in the annals of the world." He expected the Confederacy to "become a nation among the nations of the earth, designed, in the hands of God, to fulfill a glorious destiny." When the going got tough, patriotism became the last refuge not of the scoundrel but of the genuinely committed soldier. "Our struggle has to be carried on desperately, and with the determination to die rather than be conquered," wrote Sandie Pendleton of Virginia during a low point in Confederate fortunes. "Our men are thinking too much of a whole skin, and too little of their country and the future. What difference does a few hours more or less here of life make in comparison with the future destiny of the people?"[7] The writer of these words was killed at Fisher's Hill.

Over and over again in Confederate letters, one finds sentences like these: "It is better to spend our all in defending our country than to be subjugated and have it taken away from us." "It is better to die than be subjugated, and I for one am ready and willing to fight to the bitter end." *Subjugated* was the favorite word for the fate worse than death that would face southern whites if the Confederacy lost the war. *Enslaved* was another frequent choice to describe that fate. "We had better all go the same way [as those who have died] than suffer the wretches who are trying to enslave us, to accomplish their ends. I prefer death to Yankee rule."[8]

Such phrases as "the holy cause of southern freedom," "duty to one's country," "death before Yankee rule," "glorious destiny," "bursting the bonds of tyranny," and the like, may come across to this post-Freudian age as mawkish posturing, romantic sentimentalism, hollow platitudes. We seldom speak or write that way anymore. Most people have not done so since World War I, which, as Ernest Hemingway and Paul Fussell have written, made such words as *glory, honor, courage, hallow, sacrifice, valor,* and *sacred* vaguely embarrassing if not mock-heroic.[9] Without question, such hackneyed phrases as "tell mother I died for my country," reported as the dying words of many a Civil War soldier, were a sentimental convention. But our cynicism about the genuineness of such sentiments is more our problem than theirs. It raises a barrier to our understanding of what I am convinced, after reading at least 25,000 letters and more than a hundred diaries of Civil War soldiers, were deeply felt convictions. That was the age of romanticism in literature, music, art, and philosophy. It was a sentimental age when strong men were not afraid to cry (or weep, as they would say), when Harriet Beecher Stowe's great novel and Stephen Foster's songs could stir genuine emotions. What seems like bathos or platitudes to us were real pathos and convictions for them.

All of the quotations I have presented here were taken from uncensored private letters and diaries. These men were not posturing for public consumption. They were not looking back from years later through a romantic haze of myth about the war. They were writing during the immediacy of their experience to explain and justify their beliefs to family members or friends who shared—or in some cases questioned—those beliefs. And how smugly can we sneer at their expressions of willingness to die for those beliefs when we know that so many of them did just that?

But one might justly ask whether most Confederate soldiers shared these convictions. The answer is yes—with some qualifications. Of 374 Confederate soldiers whose letters and diaries I have read, two-thirds expressed patriotic motives. The proportion that discoursed in more depth on ideological issues such as liberty, constitutional rights, resistance to tyranny, and so on was smaller—40 percent. That does not mean that those who made no references to these matters were unmoved by them. By their nature, most personal letters or diary entries were descriptive rather than reflective, concerned with day-to-day events in the army and at home—with the weather, food, sickness, and other mundane concerns. The dominant themes in letters were homesickness and a longing for peace. Yet as much as they wanted to return to their families, many of these soldiers would have echoed the words of a Texas officer who wrote to his wife in 1863 that even though "I am sick of war" and "no gratification could exceed that of my being safe at home with you," nevertheless "were the contest just commenced I would willingly undergo it again for the sake of . . . our country's independence [so I can] . . . point with pride your children to their father as one who fought for their liberty & freedom." [10]

How representative is this sample of 374 soldiers? They came from all states of the South in roughly the same proportions as did all Confederate soldiers. Their average age was about the same as that of the army as a whole. But in other respects the sample is not representative in the sense that a modern Gallup Poll or survey questionnaire is designed to represent proportionately all the relevant groups in a given population. This sample of soldiers is, of course, biased toward the groups most likely to write letters or diaries and to save them for posterity to read. By definition, the 15 to 20 percent of Confederate soldiers who were illiterate are not included. An overlapping category, the unskilled laborers who constituted about 8 percent of Confederate soldiers, are also unrepresented. Skilled laborers and foreign-born soldiers are decidedly underrepresented. Although the sample includes a substantial number of yeoman farmers, they too are underrepresented. On the other hand, the planter class and the professional classes—especially lawyers—are overrepresented. Therefore slaveholders are also overrepresented. Whereas about one-third of all Confederate soldiers came from slaveholding families, a little more than two-thirds of my sample whose slaveholding status is known did so. Thus the groups most likely to express strong ideological convictions are overrepresented in the sample: for example, 75 percent of the soldiers from slaveholding families avowed strong patriotic convictions, compared with 42 percent among non-slaveholders; 43 percent of those from slaveholding families expressed ideological motives, compared with 27 percent of the nonslaveholding soldiers.

The sample also provides an imperfect cross-section of the internal structure of the Confederate army. It overrepresents those who enlisted during the first year of the war, before conscription went into effect, and underrepresents conscripts, substitutes, and those who volunteered only to avoid being drafted. There was a marked difference between these two groups in the level of patriotic and ideological conviction. Among yeoman farmers, for example, 56 percent of those who enlisted in the first year of the war asserted patriotic sentiments, compared with only 14 percent of those who came into the army after conscription was enacted. The least enthusiastic soldiers were nonslaveholding farmers in their thirties who were drafted in 1862 and forced to leave behind a wife and several small children. Their bitterness became even more acute after the Twenty-Negro Law in October, 1862, exempted from the draft one white man on every plantation of twenty or more slaves. This law exacerbated the class tensions that a number of historians have identified as undermining Confederate unity and morale.

I found less evidence of the "rich man's war / poor man's fight" attitude in soldiers' letters than I expected, given the prevalence of this theme in recent scholarship. But I did find some, such as the dirt farmer in the 60th North Carolina who complained in an 1863 letter to his wife that "this is a Rich mans Woar But the poor man has to doo the fiting," or another farmer, drafted into the 57th North Carolina, who lamented that "I could be at home if it warent for a fiew big rulers who I cannot help but blame for it. . . . These big fighting men cant be got out to fight as easy as to make speaches . . . all they care for is to keep the poor men run away from home and they lay at home feesting on the good things of the land . . . while we poor soldiers are foursed away from home and dare not return if we do we are liable to be shot to death." [11]

These negative sentiments seem to have been stronger among soldiers from North Carolina than from any other state. This may help to explain why the desertion rate was highest in North Carolina regiments. In general, a larger proportion of soldiers from lower-South cotton states expressed strong patriotic and ideological motives than of those from the upper South. The contrast between South Carolina and North Carolina soldiers was especially notable: 82 percent from South Carolina avowed patriotic convictions, compared with 47 percent from North Carolina.

These regional and state contrasts fit with the data cited earlier showing a greater degree of ideological commitment among soldiers from slaveholding than from nonslaveholding families, for a higher percentage of families in the Deep South owned slaves than in the upper South. This pattern is also confirmed by a comparison of officers and enlisted men. The proportion of slaveholders among officers was almost twice that among enlisted men. The disparity in their degree of avowed ideological and patriotic convictions was almost as great. And here also is another and perhaps the most serious distortion in the sample: whereas some 10 or 12 percent of all Confederate soldiers served as officers for at least half of their time in the army, 47 percent of my sample did so. In that respect, as in those of wealth, slaveholding, occupation, and education, the sample is biased toward those who had the largest stake in the Confederacy and were therefore most prone to have strong ideological convictions. This bias cannot be helped, for it reflects the selectivity of the evidence available to the historian who seeks to get inside the minds of those men.

In one final way is the sample unrepresentative. But this bias may go a long way to neutralize the others. The title of this book is *What They Fought For*. Let me emphasize the second and third words of that title. Who were the *they* that *fought*? Civil War soldiers—officers and men, Union and Confederate alike—agreed that about half of the men on the rolls did nearly all of the real fighting. The remainder were known, in Civil War slang, as beats or dead-beats, skulkers, sneaks, stragglers, or coffee-coolers. They "played off" (shirked) or played sick when battle impended. They seemed to melt away when bullets started flying, only to reappear the next day. Some deserted for good. Some really were sick much of the time. Others got what combat soldiers called "bombproof" jobs a safe distance behind the lines—headquarters clerk, quartermaster sergeant, wagon-train guard, teamster, hospital attendant, and the like. My sample is biased toward genuine fighting soldiers. What is the evidence for that statement? The best way to tell who really fought is to look at casualty rates—the fighting regiments were those with the highest casualties; the fighting soldiers were those most likely to get killed. Some 11 or 12 percent of all Confederate soldiers were killed or mortally wounded in action; no less than 29 percent of the men in my sample died that way. This rather startling bias in the sample may have occurred because those who did the fighting came disproportionately from the same groups as the sample. But the main explanation probably is that the families of soldiers killed in action were the most likely to

preserve their memory and therefore their letters for posterity—and for the historian. In any case, if we are interested
in what the *they* who did most of the fighting thought they
were fighting for, the unrepresentativeness of the sample may
help us to answer the question.

The concepts of southern nationalism, liberty, self-government, resistance to tyranny, and other ideological purposes I
quoted earlier all have a rather abstract quality. But for many
Confederate soldiers these abstractions took a concrete, visceral form: the defense of home and hearth against an invad-
ing enemy. This purpose in turn became transformed for
many southern soldiers into hatred and a desire for revenge.
These were purposes and motives that, for obvious reasons, functioned much more powerfully for Confederate than
for Union soldiers. "We are fighting for matters real and
tangible . . . our property and our homes," wrote a Texas
private in 1864, "they for matters abstract and intangible."
A Tennessee lieutenant insisted that "the yankees are sacri-
ficing their lives for nothing; we ours for home, country, and
all That is dear and sacred. . . . Every one seems to know
that his life liberty and property are at stake, hence we never
can be whipped."[12] A young Alabama soldier agreed that
"when a Southron's home is threatened the spirit of resistance
is irrepressable," and one of the Confederacy's numerous
gentleman privates—men who enlisted in the ranks despite
their wealth and social status—a thirty-two-year-old Virginia
planter, declared two weeks before he was killed at Malvern
Hill that to drive "the insolent invader . . . from the soil polluted by their footsteps . . . has something of the glorious in
it, that appeals to other feelings than those of patriotism and
duty."[13]
Military analysts who have studied the will of armies to
fight confirm this southern conviction: defense of the home-

land is one of the most powerful combat motivations.[14] Some northern soldiers conceded this truth. They "fight like Devils in tophet," an Illinois sergeant wrote of the Confederates in 1862, because they were "fighting to keep an enemy out of [their] own neighborhood & protect [their] property. . . . Not that I consider their cause just but, right or wrong, if we thot or believed we was right it would be the same to us." Two years later an officer, also from Illinois, made the same point in a letter to his wife: "They are fighting from different motives from us. We are fighting for the Union . . . a high and noble sentiment, but after all a sentiment. They are fighting for independence and are animated by passion and hatred against invaders. . . . It makes no difference whether the cause is just or not. You can get up an amount of enthusiasm that nothing else will excite."[15]

The antebellum propaganda war between North and South had created in southern minds an image of the hated Yankees as an amalgam of money-grubbing mudsill Black Republican abolitionist Goths and Vandals. Well before significant Union invasions of the South, Confederate soldiers' letters bristled with these negative stereotypes. The following quotations are all from letters written during the first months of the war. It is "a glorious mission . . . to defend our homes from the spoiler," from "hordes of Northern Hessians," to fight "in defence of innocent girls & women from the fangs of lecherous Northern hirelings," or in "defiance to the Vandal hordes, who would desecrate and pollute our Southern Soil." "I will never stand by and see my native soil polluted by a horde of Abolition incendiaries" or for that matter by the "lowest and most contemptible race upon the face of God's earth," "the theiving hordes of Lincoln."[16]

If these phrases seem like clichés, they nevertheless had real meaning to those who wrote them. The same was true of the numerous expressions of intent to defend southern womanhood from the "vile and inhuman wretches" of the North. A young Texas private with a sense of humor wrote to his parents from Memphis, where his regiment had gone after fighting at Pea Ridge, that he had met two "beautifull women" who had given him a bouquet of flowers. He put the bouquet in the muzzle of his musket and bid farewell, thinking "as I sped my way . . . the mistery is solved . . . what are we fighting for why 'By George' we are fighting for the women." [17] Men with wives and sisters felt this obligation a good deal more seriously, filling their letters with references to protecting "the fair daughters of my own native state . . . from Yankee outrage and atrocity," from the "varlet's tread," the "fiendish vandals" and "despoiler of Southern homes," shielding "the loved ones who call upon me to defend their homes from pillage." [18] "Do you suppose we are going to submit to see our wives etc. insulted for all future by brutes they would send among us?" a North Carolina colonel wrote his wife in 1861 with a rhetorical question which he promptly answered: "So long as we have such wives, mothers, and sisters to fight for so long will this struggle continue until finally our freedom will be acknowledged." [19]

This conviction that they fought for their homes and women gave many Confederate soldiers remarkable staying power in the face of adversity. "My dear be a brave woman to the last," wrote a Shenandoah Valley farmer serving in the 10th Virginia Cavalry to his wife when their home was threatened by the invaders. "I intend to fight them to the last . . . I will kill them as long as I live even if peace is made I never will get done with them." A gentleman private in the 21st Mississippi told his mother that "the life of a soldier is a hard one & no amount of description can convey the most remote idea of the hardships. . . . Still . . . I am perfectly content to remain five years or until there is not a Yankee south of the Mason & Dixon's line." Another planter's son, a sergeant in the 16th Mississippi with two brothers in the same regiment, also detested the drudgery of an enlisted man's lot. Nevertheless, he wrote to his mother in 1862, "I joyfully embrace it as a means of repelling a dastardly, plundering, oppressive, and cowardly foe from our homes and borders. . . . And cheerfully I determine never to lay down my rifle as long as a Yankee remains on Southern soil." [20]

This Mississippi sergeant concluded his letter with the words: "Mother I am getting to hate the Yankees in earnest." As the war escalated in fury, mounting Confederate casualties and loss of property, including slaves, caused this flame of hatred to burn ever more brightly. Bitter enmity and a desire for revenge became the consuming passion of many Confederate soldiers—motives that, like defense of home and hearth, operated much more powerfully for them than for Union soldiers.

Vengeance for comrades cut down by Yankee bullets became an obsession with some Confederates. When the popular colonel of Terry's Texas rangers was killed in a skirmish, a sergeant in the troop reported that "the men were too much exasperated after the death of our colonel to take prisoners—they were shot down." Another Texan, a captain, wrote his wife to teach their children "a bitter and unrelenting hatred to the Yankee race" that "have invaded our country and devastated it . . . [and] murdered our best citizens. . . . If any luckless Yank should unfortunately come into my way he need not petition for mercy. If he does I'le give him lead if he ask for bread. . . . [I intend] to *Massacre* the last one of them that ever has or may hereafter place his unhallowed feet upon the soil of our sunny South." [21]

Texans seemed particularly ferocious on this subject, at least rhetorically. But soldiers from other states were not far behind—especially states that experienced northern occupation and confiscation of property. A Virginia cavalry officer and planter who learned that his slaves had run off to Union lines angrily denounced the Yankees as "a nation of thieves and robbers. . . . [I] am the more willing to kill as many of them as God in his providence will permit me." The most unrelenting rhetoric of revenge came from a Louisiana cavalry sergeant, a schoolteacher before the war, whose pen was at least as sharp as his saber. He had enlisted for patriotic reasons, he wrote his wife in 1863, but by the time Vicksburg and Port Hudson had fallen the "only one thing" that kept him going was "absolute hatred of . . . the hyperborean vandals with whom we are waging a war for existence. . . . The Thugs of India will not bear a comparison to my hatred and destruction of them when opportunity offers. . . . I expect to murder every Yankee I ever meet when I can do so with impunity if I live a hundred years and peace is made in six months. . . . I don't intend ever to take any prisoners. I think anybody who should see the destruction they have caused in this country would applaud the resolution." [22]

Some Confederate soldiers demanded an eye-for-an-eye retaliation for the burning of southern cities. A lieutenant in the 4th Virginia declared that "I for one should like to apply with my own hands a torch to Philadelphia or New York that would level either of those proud cities with the ground." A sergeant in the 8th Georgia on his way into Pennsylvania in June, 1863, voiced the conviction that "we [should] take horses; burn houses; and commit every depredation possible upon the men of the North . . . slay them like wheat before the sythe in harvest time. I certainly love to live to kill the base usurping vandals. if it is a sin to hate them; then I am guilty of the unpardonable one." As matters turned out, he had little chance to burn houses or slay Yankees like wheat; he was himself killed in the first exchange of fire at Devil's Den. Another Virginian, though, a captain in one of the regiments that burned Chambersburg, Pennsylvania in 1864, described that event with pleasure in a letter to a cousin: "Our men soon became drunk & mad for plunder. Some would come to a man's house with a torch & demand $500 or so, or else they wd. fire his house. This he wd. give, and fancy himself safe, when another would come, and make a similar demand. This was continued untill all his money was gone, when the last party would set fire to it. . . . It was one of the best strokes we have ever inaugurated, its effects have been most beneficial."[23]

In some Confederates this passion became almost pathological. A Maryland-born officer in Longstreet's corps, a grandson of the architect Benjamin Latrobe (who helped design the United States Capitol and the White House), directed the artillery fire of ten Confederate guns on Marye's Heights at the battle of Fredericksburg. Afterward he rode over the battlefield and, as he described the experience in his diary, "enjoyed the sight of hundreds of dead Yankees. Saw much of the work I had done in the way of severed limbs, decapitated bodies, and mutilated remains of all kinds. Doing my soul good. Would that the whole Northern Army were as such & I had my hand in it." Similarly, a Texas officer rode over the Chickamauga battlefield viewing "the black and swollen [Yankee] corpses that will never be buried and whose bones will be bleached by the pelting rains of the coming winter," and "it actually done me good to see them laying dead, and every one else that I heard expressed [the same] opinion."[24] The gentleman private in the 21st Mississippi quoted earlier wrote to his parents after Antietam that there were hundreds of dead Yankees lying in the sector of the battlefield controlled by the Confederates before they retreated. "Tell Miss Anna," he wrote of his sister, "that I thought of collecting her a peck of Yankee finger nails to make her a sewing basket of as she is ingenious at such things but I feared I could not get them to her." A Virginia cavalryman had better luck when he camped on the battlefield of Brandy Station ten weeks after the great cavalry battle there and found himself "laying on Yankee bones" at the very spot where his regiment had fought. He wrote his wife that his brother Preston, in the same regiment, "is now making a ring of some portion of the leg bone of the dead yankee." [25]

Perhaps the ultimate in vindictiveness was expressed by an officer in an artillery battery defending Charleston, who was cheered by news of the burning of Chambersburg. "I long to hear," he wrote his fiancée, like him a member of a prominent low-country family, "that we are paying the Yankees off in the same coin we have been enduring for the last 4 years—burn! and slay! until Ft. Pillow with all its fancied horrors shall appear as insignificant as a schoolboy's tale." A month later, after Sherman's capture of Atlanta, many of the Union prisoners at Andersonville were moved to Charleston. The South Carolinian wrote again to his fiancée that "I never saw a worse looking set than the Yankee prisoners. They have all wasted away from starvation and are fortunately dying rapidly. . . . That is much better than exchanging them." Yellow fever had broken out in Charleston, and "if it only gets among those 15,000 [prisoners] encamped on the race course it will make them beautifully less." [26]

I do not mean to suggest that such sentiments animated most Confederates. It is true that as the war ground on and devastated a widening swath of the South, the initial patriotism and ideological commitment of many Confederate soldiers became transmuted into hatred and a passion for revenge. But for others their initial idealism, even if intensified by more visceral emotions, persisted to the end. Confederate soldiers' letters and diaries continued in 1864 and even into 1865 to abound with such expressions as this "gigantic struggle for liberty," for "the great Democratic principles of States' Rights and States' Sovereignty," for "the dear rights of freemen" against "tyranny and oppression," a cause "made a thousand times dearer by the sacrifice it has cost and is costing us."[27] At a low point in Confederate morale in 1864, a Mississippi private insisted that "the old Troops are not as near whiped as the citizens at home. . . . Let [the war] be long or short meat or no meat shoes or no shoes [we are] Resolved to fight it out . . . for the sake of liberty . . . if we give it up now we will certainly be the most degraded people on earth." A Louisiana cavalryman believed that a Yankee triumph would be "more galling in its tyranny than the darkest horror under which Ireland or Poland has ever groaned," and a Mississippi officer feared it would mean descent "to a depth of degradation immeasurably below that of the Helots of Greece."[28]

We must give the last word to an Alabama lieutenant who exulted in the name of Rebel. "We should be proud of [that] noble name," he wrote in December, 1864. "George Washington . . . Thomas Jefferson, Patrick Henry, and 'Light Horse' Harry Lee . . . were all Rebels. . . . Our martyred Saviour was called *seditious,* and I may be pardoned if I rejoice that I am a Rebel."[29]

Could Union soldiers match this intensity of ideological conviction? The next chapter will address that question.

2

"The Best Government on God's Footstool"

One of the questions often asked a Civil War historian is, "Why did the North fight?" Southern motives seem easier to understand. Confederates fought for independence, for their property and way of life, for their very survival as a nation. But what did Yankees fight for? Why did they persist through four years of the bloodiest conflict in American history, costing 360,000 northern lives—not to mention 260,000 southern lives and untold destruction of resources? Puzzling over this question in 1863, Confederate War Department clerk John Jones wrote in his diary: "Our men *must* prevail in combat, or lose their property, country, freedom, everything. . . . On the other hand the enemy, in yielding the contest, may retire into their own country, and possess everything they enjoyed before the war began."[1]

If that was true, why did the Yankees keep fighting? We can find much of the answer in Abraham Lincoln's notable speeches: the Gettysburg Address, his first and second inaugural addresses, the peroration of his message to Congress on December 1, 1862. But we can find even more of the answer in the wartime letters and diaries of the men who did the fighting. Confederates who said that they fought for the same goals as their forebears of 1776 would have been surprised by the intense conviction of northern soldiers that *they* were upholding the legacy of the American Revolution.

"We fight for the blessings bought by the blood and treasure of our Fathers," wrote an enlisted man from Missouri to his parents in 1861. "I will fight till I die if necessary for the liberties which you have so long enjoyed." A Michigan soldier told his younger brother that he fought against "Traitors who sought to tear down and break into fragments the glorious temple that our forefathers reared with blood and tears."[2] A New Jersey officer declared that "the man who doesn't give hearty support to our bleeding country in this day of our country's trial is not worthy to be a descendant of our forefathers. . . . We will be held responsible before God if we don't do our part in helping to transmit this boon of civil and religious liberty down to succeeding generations." An Illinois farm boy whose parents had opposed his enlistment asked them tartly: "Should We the youngest and brightest nation of all the earth bow to traters and forsake the graves of our Fathers?" He answered his own question: "No no never."[3]

The theme of parallel sacrifice with the patriots of 1776 punctuated the letters of many Union soldiers. An officer in the 101st Ohio wrote in December, 1862, that "our fathers in coldest winter, half clad marked the road they trod with crimson streams from their bleeding feet that we might enjoy the blessings of a free government." Likewise, "our business in being here [is] to lay down our lives if need be for our country's cause." Two weeks later he was killed in the battle of Stones River. A young Michigan private was also killed in action not long after he wrote a letter to his uncle describing the hardships of a soldier's life. But "did the revolutionary patriots in valley forge," he asked rhetorically, "complain [when] they had to march in the snow with there bare feet and to stand the cold twenty degrees below zero without blankets? . . . We will show our fathers and mothers wifes sisters brothers and sweethearts that we are" worthy of that heritage.[4]

Some of those wives, however, told their soldier husbands that they had a greater responsibility to their present families than to the founding fathers. In response to such letters from wives, a good many Union soldiers wrote as did an Ohio lieutenant: "Our Fathers made this country, we, their children are to save it . . . and you should . . . experience a laudable pride in the part your [husband and brothers] are now taking to suppress the greatest rebellion the history of the world has ever witnessed. . . . Why denounce the war when the interest at stake is so vital? . . . Without Union & peace our freedom is worthless . . . our children would have no warrant of liberty. . . . [If] our Country be numbered among the things that were but are not, of what value will be house, family, and friends?" Another Ohio soldier, whose wife complained repeatedly of the burdens of raising three children while worrying about his fate, asked her to "bear your trouble with good cheer. . . . It only gives another trouble on my mind to know that you are so discontented. . . . If you esteem me with a true woman's love you will not ask me to disgrace myself by deserting the flag of our Union a flag that is as dear as life to me. . . . No it will never do, cheer up and . . . remember that thousands went forth and poured out their lifs blood in the Revolution to establish this government; and twould be a disgrace to the whole American people if she had not noble sons enough who had the spirit of seventy six in their hearts." Justifying to *his* wife a decision to stay in the army after more than a year's fighting instead of accepting a medical discharge, a thirty-three-year-old Minnesota sergeant, father of three children, wrote home from an army hospital where he was recovering from exhaustion: "My grandfather fought and risked his life to bequeath to his posterity . . . the glorious

Institutions" now threatened by "this infernal rebellion. . . . It is not for you and I, or us & our dear little ones, alone, that I was and am willing to risk the fortunes of the battle-field, but also for the sake of the country's millions who are to come after us."[5]

But why did these soldiers think that the "infernal rebellion" jeopardized the survival of the glorious republic? Why could they not, as Confederate War Department clerk John Jones suggested, merely return home to a northern nation and leave the South alone so that the two republics could live in peace as dual heirs of the Revolution? Because, said northern soldiers almost as if in echo of Abraham Lincoln, once admit that a state can secede at will, and republican government by majority rule would come to an end. The dis—United States would fragment into several petty, squabbling autocracies, proving the contention of European monarchists and re-actionaries that this harebrained experiment in democracy could not last. Government of the people, by the people, for the people would perish from the earth. Many Union soldiers voiced with extraordinary passion the conviction that pres-ervation of the *United* States as "the beacon light of liberty & freedom to the human race," in the words of a thirty-five-year-old Indiana sergeant, was indeed the last, best hope for the survival of republican liberties in the Western world.[6]

"I do feel that the liberty of the world is placed in our hands to defend," wrote a Massachusetts private to his wife in 1862, "and if we are overcome then farewell to freedom." If "traitors be allowed to overthrow and break asunder ties most sacred—costing our forefathers long years of blood and toil," agreed a Connecticut enlisted man in 1863, then "all the hope and confidence of the world in the capacity of men for self government will be lost . . . and perhaps be followed by a long night of tyranny."[7] In 1863 on the second anniver-sary of his enlistment, a thirty-three-year-old Ohio private wrote in his diary that he had not expected the war to go on so long, but no matter how much longer it took it must be prosecuted "for the great principles of liberty and self government at stake, for should we fail, the onward march of Liberty in the Old World will be retarded at least a century, and Monarchs, Kings and Aristocrats will be more powerful against their subjects than ever." After Lee's surrender at Appomattox, a fifty-one-year-old New Jersey colonel who had fought the entire four years wrote to his wife that "we [can] return to our homes with the proud satisfaction that it has been our privilege to live and take part in the struggle that has decided for all time to come that Republics are not a failure."[8]

All of these quotations are from native-born soldiers, many of whose ancestors did fight in the Revolution. Yet one quarter of the white soldiers in the Union army were foreign born. They are proportionately underrepresented in my sample, and some of those whose letters I have read were not particularly ideological. Others were, however—especially on the theme of the Union as a beacon light of liberty for the oppressed in their homelands. In 1864 a forty-year-old Ohio corporal who had been born in England wrote to his wife after he had reenlisted for a second three-year hitch: "If I do get hurt I want you to remember that it will be not only for my Country and my Children but for Liberty all over the World that I risked my life, for if Liberty should be crushed here, what hope would there be for the cause of Human Progress anywhere else?"[9]

Irish-American soldiers drew some of the clearest parallels between their fight for the Union and the struggle for liberty in the old country. A thirty-three-year-old Irish-born carpenter, a private in the 28th Massachusetts of the famous Irish Brigade, angrily rebuked both his wife in Boston and his father-in-law back in Ireland for questioning his judgment in fighting for the Black Republican Lincoln administration. "This is my country as much as the man who was born on the soil," he wrote in 1863. "I have as much interest in the maintenance of . . . the integrity of the nation as any other man. . . . This is the first test of a modern free government in the act of sustaining itself against internal enemys . . . if it fail then the hopes of milions fall and the designs and wishes of all tyrants will succeed the old cry will be sent forth from the aristocrats of europe that such is the common lot of all republics. . . . Irishmen and their decendents have . . . a stake in [this] nation. . . . America is Irlands refuge Irlands last hope destroy this republic and her hopes are blasted." [10]

Like Lincoln, many northern soldiers saw secession as a deadly challenge to the foundation of law and order on which all societies must rest if they are not to degenerate into anarchy. "The central idea of secession," said Lincoln, "is the essence of anarchy." Southern states had seceded in response to Lincoln's election by a constitutional majority in a fair vote held under rules accepted by all parties. To reject this outcome would destroy the basis of constitutional democracy, said Lincoln, and "fly to anarchy or to despotism." [11]

Echoes of these words can be found in many soldiers' letters. We are "fighting for the maintenance of law and order," they wrote, "to assert the strength and dignity of the government" against the threat of "dissolution, anarchy, and ruin." [12] A New York lieutenant and an Iowa colonel agreed that "constitutional liberty cannot survive the loss of unity in the government. . . . If [secession] can prosper under such auspices surely the downfall of civilization like that which devastated Rome has returned to dessolate the world." [13]

Officers from upper- or middle-class backgrounds were the most likely to voice this law-and-order theme. But a good many enlisted men from humbler circumstances did so as well. A twenty-three-year-old printer from Philadelphia, a private in the 71st Pennsylvania wounded while helping to repel Pickett's assault at Gettysburg, wrote to his father that any sacrifice was worth the cost, "for what is home with all its endearments, if we have not a country freed from every vestige of the anarchy, and the tyrannical and blood thirsty despotism which threatens on every side to overwhelm us?" To an Ohio blacksmith and miller, the cause for which he fought as a private in the 70th Ohio was "the cause of the constitution and law," he wrote in 1863. "Admit the right of the seceding states to break up the Union at pleasure . . . and how long will it be before the new confederacies created by the first disruption shall be resolved into still smaller fragments and the continent become a vast theater of civil war, military license, anarchy and despotism? Better settle it at whatever cost and settle it forever." [14]

Like Johnny Reb, though, Billy Yank most often expressed what he fought for in words of simple patriotism. We "have gone forth to defend this Country in this her hour of peril," wrote a young Connecticut recruit who would lose his life in the contest. A Union corporal from Missouri declared that "No one loves wife or family more than I. Yet my country has claims upon me strong as that of home or family." The mother of a corporal in the 8th Pennsylvania Cavalry was probably not gratified by a letter from her son that listed his duties in the following order of priority: "first my God, second my country, third my mother. Oh my country, how my heart bleeds for your welfare. If this poor life of mine could save you, how willingly would I make the sacrifice." [15] This statement is saved from bathos by our knowledge that he did indeed sacrifice his life in one of the last battles of the war, at Dinwiddie Court House on March 31, 1865. A similar fate overtook a deputy sheriff from Minnesota; he was killed at Gettysburg a month after writing to a friend that he was prepared to give his life "for the purpose of crushing this d——d rebellion and to support the best government on God's footstool." And a fifty-four-year-old farmer from up-state New York was killed in the battle of Plymouth not long after he had written his wife: "My country, glorious country, if we have only made it truly the land of the free . . . I count not my life dear unto me if only I can help that glorious cause along." [16]

Glorious. Sacrifice. Hearts bleeding for the welfare of the country. These are the words that Ernest Hemingway mocked in *A Farewell to Arms*. We would justly mock them if we heard them today. Even in the 1860s such phrases in a Fourth of July speech or at a recruiting rally might evoke a cynical guffaw. But these words occurred in letters to loved ones from men on the front lines who did give their lives. They must be taken seriously. I remained skeptical about this even after reading hundreds of such statements, both Union and Confederate. But I was finally converted when I encountered the letters of two Quaker brothers, farmers from New York State, whose ideological convictions overcame their pacifism and caused them to enlist, leaving behind a widowed mother. "If I die for the cause of the Unity entire of this government," wrote the older brother (age twenty-six) to her, "that is the way a man should die, for die he must, and a few years more or less don't make much difference. . . . A man in fighting for liberty . . . can realize that he died to save something better than life." Less than two months later he was killed at Gettysburg. The younger brother consoled their mother that "he is laid a sacrifice on the altar of Liberty . . . with his face toward the enemies of freedom." But "Oh, God! Thy price for freedom is a DEAR ONE!" Three months later the younger brother also died, in Libby prison after having been captured in a skirmish. Their words were not mawkish melodrama; they *meant* what they said. [17]

But the same questions that we asked about Confederate

soldiers must be asked here. How typical were these expressions of patriotic and ideological convictions? And how representative is the sample? The answer to the first question is the same as it was for Confederates. Of 562 Union soldiers whose letters or diaries I have read, 67 percent voiced simple but strong patriotic convictions and 40 percent went further, expressing ideological purposes such as liberty, democracy, majority rule, constitutional law and order, and survival of the Revolutionary legacy of republican government as the causes for which they fought. This compares with 66 and 40 percent in these two categories for Confederate soldiers— virtually identical with the Union percentages.

There was one difference between Yankees and Rebels, however. Among Confederates, 82 percent of the officers, compared with 52 percent of enlisted men, avowed patriotic motives; 52 percent of the officers but only 28 percent of the enlisted men went further and discoursed upon ideological goals. The difference between officers and enlisted men was smaller for Union soldiers: 78 percent of officers and 61 percent of enlisted men expressed patriotism; 49 and 36 percent, respectively, advanced various ideological themes, including opposition to slavery. Moreover, officers are less overrepresented in the Union sample than in the Confederate: 35 percent of the Union sample were officers for at least half of their service, compared with 47 percent of the Confederate sample.

What is the significance of this? Using army rank as a surrogate for class, it means that patriotic and ideological convictions were shared more evenly across class lines in the Union army than among Confederate soldiers. This interpretation is confirmed by other data in my samples. Among the Confederates, the highest-status groups—members of planter families and of slaveholding professional families—expressed ideological convictions at twice the rate of nonslaveholding soldiers. In the Union army the disparity between comparable groups—professionals and high white-collar occupations on one hand and low white-collar and blue-collar workers on the other—was much less, only about 25 percent.

To summarize: In both the Union and Confederate samples, soldiers expressed about the same degree of patriotic and ideological convictions. But the larger disproportion of officers in the Confederate sample skews that percentage upward, and the higher degree of such convictions among enlisted men and lower-status groups in the Union sample compared with their Confederate counterparts means a greater democratization of ideological purpose among Union soldiers. What impact that difference had on morale and fighting effectiveness is hard to say. It may explain the dogged determination that sustained Union soldiers through four long years of fighting in enemy territory against a foe sustained by the more concrete motive of defending that territory. It also probably reflects the higher literacy rate, broader education, and greater degree of political awareness in the North than in the South.

But let us not overstate this point. For one thing, although my Union sample is somewhat more representative of the class spectrum of the army as a whole than the Confederate sample, it is still skewed toward officers and upper-strata occupations. Some 45 percent of the men in the Union sample had held professional or white-collar jobs in civilian life, compared with about 11 percent for the Union army as a whole. And only 3 percent of the sample were unskilled laborers, compared with 16 percent of all Union soldiers. The 7 or 8 percent of white Union soldiers who were illiterate are not represented in the sample, nor are the 70 percent or more of the black soldiers who could not read or write. In fact, only 2 of the 562 men in the sample were black, so it is impossible to say much about the ideological convictions of the 9 percent of Union soldiers who were black except to state the truism that they were aware of fighting for the freedom of their race. The most important underrepresented category is foreign-born soldiers: only 8 percent of the northern soldiers in the sample were born abroad, compared with some 24 percent in the Union army as a whole. Particularly underrepresented are Irish and German Catholics, who constituted 11 or 12 percent of the army but only 2 percent of my sample. The actual proportion of immigrants in my sample may be slightly larger than this, for I do not have information on the nativity of everyone, and some of the unknowns may have been born abroad. Nevertheless, immigrants are clearly underrepresented, and those least enthusiastic about northern war aims—Irish and German Catholics—are the most underrepresented, despite my quotation earlier of an Irish soldier.

Finally, as in the Confederate sample, the draftees, substitutes, bounty men, soldiers who enlisted to escape the draft, and deserters are radically underrepresented. But in the Union army as in the Confederate, these individuals were the least likely to do much fighting, whereas the *they* who really *fought* are overrepresented in the sample. Again this is demonstrated by casualty figures: just over 5 percent of all Union soldiers and sailors were killed or mortally wounded in action, but 17 percent of the men in the sample suffered this fate. An ideologically committed Illinois sergeant who was later killed in action told his fiancée in 1863 that "the *best, truest,* and *bravest* of the nation" went to the front and got killed, while the "beats" did their best to avoid combat. "A 'beat,'" another Union soldier explained to his brother, "is one who plays sick, shirks duty . . . and is always missing in a fight. The beats of a regiment sometimes number one half."[18] A Missouri sergeant said that bounty men and substitutes were usually found among the beats, for "it is the caus that makes a man fight . . . and they have not much love for the union." A Massachusetts corporal was killed in action not long after he wrote home: "Mother if all our army felt as I feel when I go into battle, the war would soon be over but I am sorry to say that we have got too many in the army that are not fighting for there country but for money and all they think of when they go into battle is how to . . . skulk behind the first stump . . . [and] keep out of danger." [19]

Most Yankees did not have the same consciousness of fighting to defend home and family that Confederates had. But this truism requires some qualification. Union soldiers from Confederate areas like East Tennessee and from border states plagued by guerrilla warfare rivaled the most bitter of Confederates in their feelings of hatred and desire for vengeance. East Tennessee Unionists driven from their homes to Kentucky, where they joined Union regiments, vowed to return and exact "eye for eye and toth for toth" in retaliation for reported Confederate atrocities. "*If I live, I will be revenged,*" wrote one East Tennessean. "Yes I will draw their blood and mutilate their dead bodies and help to send their souls to hell." [20] An Ohio captain serving with West Virginia Unionists expressed awe at their animosity toward Rebels. "Hate rankled in their breasts," he wrote his wife. "Oh, how strong is this passion, this desire for revenge." The bushwhacking civil war in Missouri fired Unionists there with a desperate belief "that it is to be a war of extermination. . . . It is life or death. . . . Union men will have to Leave or Pitch in and Kill as Many secesh as they can before Thay Kill [us]." [21]

Robert E. Lee's invasions of Union states in 1862 and again in 1863 produced northern echoes of southern calls for defense of home and family. A Pennsylvania soldier from a farm near Gettysburg was convinced that he was "defending my Mother and Home and Country." A cavalry trooper from Maine in the Army of the Potomac wrote from Pennsylvania in July, 1863, that "here men will fight with twice the courage and determination than they will in Virginia."[22] A semiliterate private in the 54th Pennsylvania, whose wife had rebuked him for thinking more of the Union than of her and the children, wrote to her with some asperity that "if the rebels would invade the north whad whoud become of you and my children . . . thay woud be perfeck slaves thay whoud be triede like a doge . . . and hour property wodden be worth a cent for thay wold take it to pay thair dates." A Michigan soldier told his wife in 1863 that he was fighting "to save our homes our Fathers & Mothers, Brothers & Sisters, Children & Wives from the curse of slavery & butchery. . . . I feel like fighting them to the last minute before I would give up & let them run over us & burn our homes & murder our friends as they would shurely do if they could get a chance."[23]

The notion of Confederate soldiers on a rampage in Michigan seems a bit farfetched. And indeed, few northern soldiers conjured up such a scenario. But this particular soldier had seen his brother killed in action almost by his side, which did not improve his opinion of Rebels. The desire to avenge comrades or relatives killed by enemy bullets burned as hotly in northern hearts as in southern. Another Wolverine, a sergeant in the 1st Michigan Cavalry, which became a crack regiment in George A. Custer's brigade, wrote to his mother in 1862 that two of his friends had been killed from ambush by guerrillas in the Shenandoah Valley. "Those that are left of us are determined to visit a terrible vengeance upon their murders. We are to take no prisoners after this." A private in the 10th Illinois whose best friend was mortally wounded at Fort Donelson wrote to his aunt after the fight: "I Went to help him up, he said oh Warden Care not for me, But go and revenge my deathe now is your time, it made me feel so desperate and strong as a lyon . . . that I fought with a more determined Will."[24] A New York lieutenant whose younger brother, a corporal in the same regiment, had been killed at

Cold Harbor, longed for a chance "to cut one of the Rebs into pieces [to] . . . pay them back." Three weeks later a Confederate counterattack on his sector of the Petersburg lines gave him his chance: "We let them get within 3 rods of us & then we jumped up & gave them a volley. O how we did mow them down. We thought of Cold Harbor & the Boys just went in as fast as they could."[25]

Some Union soldiers avowed a more abstract motive of revenge for Confederate atrocities elsewhere, even the Fort Pillow massacre. Whether or not Billy Yank liked black soldiers personally, he identified with the uniform they wore. A Wisconsin soldier with Sherman's army in Georgia wrote to his fiancée that when his regiment charged Confederate works at Resaca, "twenty-three of the rebs surrendered but the boys asked them if they remembered Fort Pillow and killed all of them. When there is no officer with us, we take no prisoners. . . . We want revenge for our brother soldiers and will have it. . . . Some of the [rebels] say they will fight as long as there is one of them left. We tell them that is what we want. We want to kill them all off and cleanse the country."[26]

As this letter suggests, punishment for treason and a determination to "clean out" the Rebels, whom they held responsible for starting the war, motivated many northern soldiers. "I want to fight the rest of my life if necessary," wrote an Illinois sergeant to his sister, "before we recognize them as anything but Rebels and traitors who must be humbled." "We have got to whip and partially exterminate the South," agreed a Massachusetts lieutenant in 1863. A Minnesota captain who had fought for three years would hear of no peace terms except "utter submission" of these "traitors to the government. . . . When they have submitted I would propose to hang the leaders and let the poor *dupes* of Soldiers go."[27]

More than a few Union soldiers drew a similar distinction between leaders and followers in the South, between an ar-

rogant "aristocracy" and the deluded common people. They
were familiar with the famous Senate speech by James Hammond of South Carolina in 1858 labeling the northern work-
ing class as mudsills. Many soldiers echoed the words of a
farmer's son in the 93d Illinois, whose two brothers also
fought in the war. All three of them itched for the "chance to
try our *Enfields* on some of their villainous hides and let a
little of that *high Blood* out of them, which I think will increase their respect for the *northern mud sills*." [28]

This feeling underlay the well-advertised resolve of Sherman's soldiers to take South Carolina apart. "No man ever
looked forward to any event with more joy," wrote an Ohio
soldier, "than did our boys to have a chance to meet the sons
of the mother of traitors, 'South Carolina.'" After leaving a
fiery trail through the state, another Ohio infantryman wrote
to his brother that "her black ruins will stand as a warning
of more terrible things to come" if the inhabitants persisted
in treason. This soldier was particularly contemptuous of the
self-styled Carolina aristocracy that "can talk of nothing but
the purity of blood of themselves & their ancestors. . . . Their
cant about aristocracy is perfectly sickening. . . . If you hear
any condemning us for what we have done, tell them for me
and for Sherman's Army, that '*we found here the authors of
all the calamities that have befallen this nation . . . and that
their punishment is light when compared with what justice
demanded.*'" [29]

The theme of punishment for treason became more preva-
lent as the war dragged on. It was the visceral counterpart of
retribution for invasion and destruction that increasingly motivated Confederate soldiers. This might seem to confirm Gerald Linderman's thesis, in his book *Embattled Courage,* that
the experiences of Civil War soldiers hardened them, causing
them to shed the ideals of those innocent days of 1861 and to
suffer "a disillusionment more profound than historians have

acknowledged." Another historian of the Union army, influenced by Linderman, maintains that "whatever idealism that the soldiers brought with them into the army faded" by the latter years of the war.[30]

This conclusion seems to conform with common sense. How could men sustain a high level of idealistic commitment through the grim experiences of disease, death, exhaustion, and frustration as the war ground on year after year? The weary cynicism of Bill Mauldin's Willie and Joe in World War II, the bitter disillusionment of the "grunt" in Vietnam, must have had their counterparts in the Civil War, especially during the lethal campaigns of 1864 and the wasting warfare of the trenches. Whose idealism could survive all that?

A good bit of evidence exists to support Linderman's contention that it did not survive. Desertion rates on both sides rose in the second half of the war. Many of the conscripts, substitutes, and bounty men who made up an increasing proportion of both armies from 1863 on were motivated marginally if at all by ideology or patriotism. The tone of soldiers' letters as well as their behavior did take on a more negative, cynical, callous, even brutal quality as time went on. Without doubt there was a decline in the romantic flag-waving rhetoric of the war's first year or two.

But the thousands of letters and scores of diaries I have read for the latter part of the war do not support the thesis of a decline in positive expressions of ideological and patriotic commitment among veterans who had enlisted in 1861 or 1862. Their belief in what they continued to call "the glorious Cause" was what kept many of them going. If anything, their searing experiences refined ideology into a purer, tougher product. This was particularly true for Union soldiers fighting far from home for seemingly more abstract goals than defense of home and hearth. Billy Yank needed an even stronger sense of ideological purpose to sustain him, especially during the summer of 1864, when war-weariness spread like a fog over the northern home front.

Many Yanks reached deep inside to find that purpose. "Amongst the survivors" in the 57th New York, wrote a lieutenant in 1864, "the excitement and enthusiasm of the early days has long since passed away, but the resolve still remains." An Ohio noncom wrote after three years of fighting: "I will confess it, I am very sick of war," but "the enthusiasm of the hour when we first enlisted, has greatly settled down to the firm resolve to do or die for our cause. . . . [Our] tough experiences have but served to endear our institutions more firmly in our minds."[31] After three years of service and as many wounds, Captain Oliver Wendell Holmes, Jr., of the 20th Massachusetts could still describe northern war aims as "the cause of the whole civilized world . . . the Christian crusade of the 19th century." A thirty-five-year-old officer from Pennsylvania wrote his wife that "sick as I am of this war and bloodshed, as much oh how much I want to be at home with my dear wife and children . . . every day I have a more religious feeling, that this war is a crusade for the good of mankind. . . . I [cannot] bear to think of what my children would be if we were to permit this Hellbegotten conspiracy to destroy this country."[32]

Writing from the trenches before Petersburg and Atlanta and from active fronts elsewhere during 1864, enlisted men echoed the theme of weariness but determination to see it through. "There is nothing pleasant" about soldiering, wrote a corporal from Ohio, but "I can endure its privations . . . for there is a *big Idea* which is at stake . . . the principles of Liberty, of Justice, and of the Righteousness which exalteth a Nation." A New York sergeant wrote to his fiancée that "I have had quite enough of this kind of life . . . yet the thought that we are doing what is right makes it easily borne."[33] A few months before he was killed at Fort Fisher, another

New York noncom wrote to his brother that "this is no time to carp at things which, compared with the success and reestablishment of the Republic, are insignificant." And in letters to his mother, an Irish-born sergeant in the 2d New Jersey Infantry declared that neither the "horrors of the battlefield [nor] the blind acts of unqualified generals" had "chilled my patriotism in the least." "We are still engaged in the same holy cause," he wrote on the third anniversary of his enlistment, "we have yet the same Country to fight for."[34]

Not all Union soldiers felt this strongly, of course. For every one who did, there was a bounty jumper or draftee or substitute or straggler or beat who cared more for money or for his own skin than he did for the cause. Such is always true of armies—but it seems to have been less true of Civil War armies. The iron resolve of genuinely dedicated Union veterans underlay the message conveyed by a dispatch from the American correspondent of the London *Daily News* to his paper in September, 1864. "I am astonished," he wrote, by "the extent and depth of the determination [of the northern people] to fight to the last. . . . They are in earnest in a way the like of which the world never saw before, silently, calmly, but desperately in earnest; and they will fight on, in my opinion, as long as they have men, muskets, powder . . . and would fight on, though the grass were growing in Wall Street."[35]

This was chilling news to southerners who had counted on a waning of the northern will to fight. Those southerners might have experienced an even colder chill could they have read the letters of northern soldiers confirming the observation of the *Daily News* correspondent. "*We must succeed,*" wrote an intensely Unionist Missouri officer to his wife in August, 1864. "If not this year, why then the next, or the next. And if it takes ten years, why then ten years it must be, for we never can give up, and have a Country and Government left." A New York lieutenant wrote from the Petersburg trenches, also in August, 1864, that "I would rather stay out here a lifetime (much as I dislike it) than consent to a division of our country."[36] Another New York officer thought it better to "carry on this war twenty years longer than to yield one iota of our rights"—although he did not make it that long, for he was killed three months after he wrote these words. A semiliterate farmer in the 66th Indiana admitted to his brother in 1864 that "I am tierd of ware . . . but not Discuraged I am moer Deturmin to Day than I ever was . . . I don't want to see the ware Stop until the . . . Stars and Strips waves over Every Precinct in America."[37]

Not only patriotism but also the idealism of 1861 persisted among many veterans, including a Pennsylvania private who wrote to his wife from a hospital after a couple of hundred miles of marching up and down the Shenandoah Valley in 1864, the last twenty-five of them in bare feet. He was ready to keep this up for years, he told her, for "I cannot believe Providence intends to destroy this Nation, this great asylum for the oppressed of all other nations and build a slave Oligarchy on the ruins thereof." A Kansas lieutenant who had spent more than a year in prison after capture at Chickamauga longed for release but, he wrote his fiancée, nevertheless did not want the war to end short of unconditional victory, for otherwise "the hope of the freedom of Nations and Millions in Europe and elsewhere [will be] driven back and obscured for ages." An Iowa officer who had risen from the ranks during three years of service while his father and younger sister had died and his brother was missing in action after the battle of Atlanta wrote to his distraught mother in September, 1864, that he could not resign his commission and come home while the war's outcome remained in doubt. "Thank God," he counseled her, "that you have children that will support the Government that *your* Father supported in the Revolution."[38]

These were some of the reasons why Yankee soldiers felt they could not merely "retire into their own country," as Confederate clerk John Jones expected them to do. But for some soldiers there was more yet that they fought for. A Massachusetts private named Emerson, who had interrupted his studies at Williams College to enlist and was wounded at Fredericksburg and again at Chancellorsville, wrote to his missionary parents in Hawaii from a hospital bed after he had been struck down a third time, by typhoid, that he was anxious to get back to the regiment to help "the holy cause for which I am fighting. . . . I say, better let us all *die* fighting for *union* and *liberty,* than to yield one inch to these 'rebel slave mongers,' as Charles Sumner justly calls them." And in 1864 an Ohio lieutenant, a carpenter by trade, wrote to his ten-year-old son complimenting him on a neatly written letter to the daddy he had scarcely seen during the past three years. "It tells me that while I am absent from home, fighting the battels of our country, trying to restore law and order, to our once peaceful & prosperous nation, and endeavoring to secure for each and every American citizen of every race, the rights garenteed to us in the Declaration of Independence . . . I have children growing up that will be worthy of the rights that I trust will be left for them." [39]

These soldiers were white, but they professed to fight for the freedom of another race as well as of their own. They were not typical of Union soldiers—but neither were they uncommon. The issue of slavery lay at the heart of what many soldiers on both sides thought they were fighting for. But it was not a simple or clear-cut issue, and for one side it threatened for a time to divide more than to unite them. The next chapter will analyze the soldiers' perceptions of the slavery issue.

3

"THE WAR WILL NEVER END UNTIL WE
END SLAVERY"

In his Second Inaugural Address, on March 4, 1865, Abraham Lincoln stated a proposition to which most historians today as well as most Americans of Lincoln's time would assent: slavery before the war had been a "powerful interest. All knew that this interest was, somehow, the cause of the war. To strengthen, perpetuate, and extend this interest was the object for which the insurgents would rend the Union, even by war." [1]

On this issue at least, the president and vice-president of the Confederacy concurred with Lincoln. In 1861 Jefferson Davis justified secession as an act of self-defense against the Black Republicans, whose purpose to exclude slavery from the territories would make "property in slaves so insecure as to be comparatively worthless . . . thereby annihilating in effect property worth thousands of millions of dollars." And in his famous "cornerstone" speech of March 21, 1861, Alexander Stephens maintained that the Republican threat to slavery was "the immediate cause of the late rupture and the present revolution" of Confederate independence. The old confederation known as the United States, Stephens continued, had been founded on the false idea that all men are created equal. The new Confederacy, by contrast, "is founded upon exactly the opposite idea; its foundations are laid, its cornerstone rests, upon the great truth that the negro is not equal to the white man; that slavery, subordination to the superior race, is his natural and normal condition. This, our new government, is the first, in the history of the world, based on this great physical, philosophical, and moral truth." [2]

Some Confederate soldiers were equally plainspoken in their avowals of slavery as the cause for which they fought. On the eve of secession, a young lawyer in Shreveport looked forward to "a great cotton slave Republic—with a future the most auspicious that ever waited on earthly government." He lived to see the rise but not the fall of this republic, for he was killed at Gettysburg. A lieutenant in the 28th Mississippi told his wife in 1863 that "this country without slave labor would be completely worthless. . . . If the negroes are freed the country . . . is not worth fighting for. . . . We can only live & exist by that species of labor: and hence I am willing to continue to fight to the last." [3] A captain in the 8th Alabama likewise vowed "to fight forever, rather than submit to freeing negroes among us. . . . [We are fighting for] rights and property bequeathed to us by our ancestors." And a Georgia officer, owner of forty slaves, reassured his wife, who in 1863 expressed doubts about the future of slavery, that if the Confederacy won the war "it is established for centuries." [4]

Several Confederate soldiers welcomed Lincoln's Emancipation Proclamation for bringing the real issue into the open. The "Proclamation is worth three hundred thousand soldiers to our Government at least," wrote a Kentucky cavalry sergeant who rode with John Hunt Morgan. "It shows exactly what this war was brought about for and the intention of its damnable authors." And a Virginia captain, a small slaveholder in the Shenandoah Valley, believed that "after Lincoln's proclamation any man that would not fight to the last ought to be hung as high as Haman." [5]

Confederate prospects for victory appeared brightest during the months after the Emancipation Proclamation, partly

because this measure divided the northern people and intensified a morale crisis in Union armies. Slave prices in the
South rose even faster than the rate of inflation during that
springtime of Confederate confidence. A number of soldiers
wrote home advising relatives to invest in slaves. The famous
"boy colonel" of the Confederacy, the planter's son Henry
Burgwyn, who became colonel of the 26th North Carolina at
the age of twenty-one, urged his father in February, 1863, to
put every cent he had into slaves. "I would buy boys & girls
from 15 to 20 years old & take care to have a majority of
girls," he wrote. "The increase in number of your negroes by
this means would repay the difference in the amount of available labor. . . . I would not be surprised to see negroes in
6 mos. after peace worth from 2 to 3000 dollars." Gettysburg
cut short his life before he could witness the collapse of his
dreams.[6]

But Gettysburg did not discourage Colonel E. Porter Alexander, Longstreet's chief of artillery, who won fame in that
battle for directing the barrage that preceded Pickett's charge.
Three weeks after the battle, Porter advised his wife to buy a
wet nurse for their twins, for "Carline & her baby wd. be a
fine *speculation* at $2000." Even as late as January, 1865, an
officer from low-country South Carolina wrote to his fiancée
that "now is the time for Uncle to buy some negro women
and children on the principle that if we don't succeed the
money won't be worth anything and if we do slaves will be
worth a 1000 times more than now."[7]

But such candid discussions of slavery were the exception
rather than the rule. Even in private letters, Confederate soldiers professed more often to fight *for* liberty and *against*
slavery—that is, against their own enslavement to the North.
"Sooner than submit to Northern Slavery, I prefer death,"
wrote a South Carolina captain to his wife in 1862, a phrase

repeated almost verbatim by many soldiers.[8] They filled their letters and diaries with references to "the ruthless invader who is seeking to reduce us to abject slavery." "The Deep still quiet peace of the grave is more desirable than Vassalage or Slavery." We must "die as free men or live as slaves"; better far "to die rather than be slaves." Such remarks are rescued from bombast by knowledge that all four men who wrote them—two lieutenants, a sergeant, and a private— were killed in action.[9]

Those soldiers were using the word *slavery* in the same sense that Americans in 1776 had used it to describe their subordination to Britain. Confederates claimed to fight for the same liberty their forefathers had won in 1783. A letter home from a Confederate Missourian used the word *liberty* five times in two sentences, and a corporal in the 9th Alabama celebrated his twentieth birthday in 1862 by writing proudly in his diary that "I am engaged in the glorious cause of liberty and justice, fighting for the rights of man—fighting for all that we of the South hold dear."[10]

Referring to the American revolutionaries, Samuel Johnson had asked sarcastically in 1775: "How is it that we hear the loudest yelps for liberty among the drivers of negroes?"[11] The question had struck an exposed nerve. Many Americans in Thomas Jefferson's time felt acutely the paradox of fighting for liberty while holding other people in slavery. There was no shortage of Yankees in 1861 to point out the same paradox in Confederate professions. "The *perfect* liberty they sigh for," said Abraham Lincoln, is "the liberty of making slaves of other people."[12] But Confederate soldiers, unlike many of their forebears of 1776, seemed unconscious of the paradox. In the countless references to liberty, freedom, justice, equal rights, and the like in their letters and diaries, I have found but one reference to any sense of inconsistency between the ideas of fighting for liberty and for slavery. A low-country

South Carolina planter's son in Hampton's Legion considered all this talk about liberty and the rights of man "simple nonsense; I for one am fighting for the maintenance of no such absurdity. . . . We are appealing to chartered rights. . . . It is insulting to the English common sense of race [to say that we] are battling for an abstract right common to all humanity. Every reflecting child will glance at the darkey who waits on him & laugh at the idea of such an 'abstract right.'"[13]

Absurdity or not, most Confederate soldiers believed that they were fighting for liberty *and* slavery, one and inseparable. A young physician from Louisville who joined the 4th Kentucky Confederate Infantry wrote that "We are fighting for our liberty, against tyrants of the North . . . who are determined to destroy slavery." Another South Carolina planter with Hampton's Legion wrote to his wife in early 1862 that he was willing to give his life "battling for Liberty and independence." Several weeks later he wrote again in consternation that his faithful body servant had run away to the Yankees. "It is very singular," he lamented, "and I cant account for it." A Georgia planter wrote to his wife in 1863 of "the arch of liberty we are trying to build"—and a few sentences later told her to sell a troublesome slave.[14] A planter's son who with two brothers fought in the 16th Mississippi wrote home in 1863 that he had been offered $3,500 for his body servant but was holding out for $4,000. When one of his brothers was killed at Cold Harbor, the soldier consoled their mother that "he died that we might live free men." In the spring of 1864 a South Carolina lieutenant who fought, as he put it, to defend "the land of liberty and freemen" told his mother that he intended to sell his no-account body servant, who then ran off before he could do so. Good riddance, said this soldier—"but [I] would rather had converted him into money."[15]

During the antebellum period many southerners had

avoided using the words *slaves* and *slavery,* preferring instead *servants* and *southern institutions.* Some Confederate soldiers kept up this practice even in private letters, referring to "our own social institutions," "the integrity of all our institutions," "the institutions of the whole South" as the cause for which they fought.[16] In 1863 a young North Carolina officer stopped for a meal in the home of a Pennsylvania farmer during the Gettysburg campaign. He described the scene to his mother: "They live in real Yankee style wife & daughters & a help doing all the work. It makes me more than ever devoted to our own Southern institutions." A Georgia lieutenant in Longstreet's corps was a little more explicit. "Pennsylvania is the greates country I ever saw in my life," he wrote his wife. "Molie if this state was a slave state and I was able to buy land here after the war you might count on living in Pennsylvania."[17]

Most of the soldiers quoted so far came from slaveholding families. They tended to emphasize the right of property in slaves as the basis of the liberty for which they fought. This motive, not surprisingly, was much less in evidence among nonslaveholding soldiers. But some of them emphasized a form of property they did own, one that was central to the liberty for which they fought. That property was their white skins, which put them on a plane of civil equality with slaveholders and far above those who did not possess that property. Herrenvolk democracy—the equality of all who belonged to the master race—was a powerful motivator for many Confederate soldiers.

Even though he was tired of the war, wrote a Louisiana soldier in 1862, "I never want to see the day when a negro is put on an equality with a white person. There is too many free niggers . . . now to suit me, let alone having four millions." A yeoman farmer from North Carolina facing the Yankees in Virginia vowed to "make them know that a white man is better than a nigger." [18] Similarly, a farmer from the Shenandoah Valley informed his fiancée that he fought to win "a free white man's government instead of living under a black republican government," and the son of another North Carolina dirt farmer said he would never stop fighting Yankees who were "trying to force us to live as the colored race." Many northern soldiers shared the bewilderment of a Wisconsin private who wrote home describing a conversation with Confederate prisoners captured in the Atlanta campaign: "Some of the boys asked them what they were fighting for, and they answered, 'You Yanks want us to marry our daughters to the niggers.'" [19]

Such sentiments were not confined to nonslaveholders. Many slaveholding soldiers also fought for white supremacy as well as for the rights of property. An Arkansas captain was enraged by the idea that if the Yankees won, his "sister, wife, and mother are to be given up to the embraces of their present 'dusky male servitors.'" After reading Lincoln's Proclamation of Amnesty and Reconstruction in December, 1863, which stipulated southern acceptance of emancipation as a condition of peace, another Arkansas soldier, a planter, wrote his wife that Lincoln not only wanted to free the slaves but also "declares them entitled to all the rights and privileges as American citizens. So imagine your sweet little girls in the school room with a black wooly headed negro and have to treat them as their equal." Likewise, a Georgia lieutenant wrote to his wife from the trenches on the Chattahoochee that if Atlanta and Richmond fell, "we are irrevocably lost and not only will the negroes be free but . . . we will all be on a common level. . . . The negro who now waits on you will then be as free as you are & as insolent as she is ignorant." [20]

It would be a mistake, however, to assume that Confederate soldiers were constantly preoccupied with this matter. In fact, only 20 percent of my sample of 374 southern soldiers explicitly voiced these proslavery convictions in their letters and diaries. Not surprisingly, the proportion of soldiers from slaveholding families expressing such a purpose was double that from nonslaveholding families—30 percent compared with 14 percent. Ironically, the proportion of Union soldiers who wrote about the slavery question was much greater, as we shall see. There is a ready explanation for this evident paradox. Emancipation was a salient issue for Union soldiers because it was controversial. Slavery was not salient for Confederate soldiers during most of the war because it was not controversial. They took slavery for granted as part of the southern way of life for which they fought, and did not feel compelled to discuss it. Although only 20 percent of the soldiers avowed explicit proslavery purposes in their letters and diaries, *none at all* dissented from that view.

None, that is, until the last months of the war. In the winter of 1863–1864 General Patrick Cleburne, a division commander in the Army of Tennessee, had proposed that the Confederate army should resolve its manpower shortage by freeing and arming slaves. This heretical suggestion had been squelched because, as one of Cleburne's fellow officers said, "its propositions contravene the principles on which we fight."[21] But it did not stay squelched. By the following winter, discussions of the matter became widespread. In February, 1865, Jefferson Davis and Robert E. Lee threw their weight behind a measure to enroll slaves in the army—with the assumption, although not the explicit authorization, that they would be freed as a reward for such service. This was a desperate move, but these were desperate times. As a Mississippi newspaper put it: "Although slavery is one of the principles that we started to fight for . . . if it proves an insurmountable obstacle to the achievement of our liberty and nationality, away with it!"[22]

After contentious debate, the Confederate Congress finally

passed the Negro soldier bill on March 13, 1865. The margin was three votes in the House and one in the Senate. This close split probably mirrored divisions among Confederate soldiers. By that time, however, so many soldiers had been killed or wounded or cut off from mail communication with their homes that the evidence of their real feelings is quite thin. For what it is worth, the opinions of a dozen soldiers divided more or less evenly between those who reluctantly supported the measure and those who angrily opposed it.

Soldiers in the former category shared the view of a Louisiana sergeant who wrote in January, 1865: "If we continue to lose ground as we have for the last 12 months, we will soon be defeated, and then slavery will be gone any way, and I think we should give up slavery and gain our independence." The son of a wealthy Georgia planter still believed that "the negro's happiest condition is in slavery," but between abolition by the Yankees and emancipation by Confederates he was willing to choose "the lesser of two evils." A Tennessee officer agreed that "slavery is lost or will be, & we had as well emancipate if we can make anything by it now. . . . We can certainly live without negroes better than with yankees and without negroes both." [23]

But such opinions encountered stiff resistance from other soldiers. A South Carolina planter's son wrote from the Petersburg trenches that this "humiliating" measure would "throw away what we have toiled so hard to maintain." A Missouri captain reported that his men believed it contrary to "what they have fought for the last four years." A sergeant in the 17th North Carolina who had served through the whole war wrote in February, 1865, that many men in his company were deserting because of the Negro soldier bill, and he was thinking of doing so himself. "Mother," he said, "I did not volunteer my services to fight for a free negroes country but to fight for A free white mans free country & I do not think I love my country well enough to fight with black soldiers."[24] The questions of whether black men would fight for the Confederacy and whether white soldiers would accept them became moot; before the experiment could be tried, the war was over.

A year before Lee surrendered at Appomattox, a southern private noted in his diary that Confederate victory was certain because "we are fighting for our property and homes; they, for the flimsy and abstract idea that a negro is equal to an Anglo American."[25] He was wrong. Few Union soldiers professed to fight for racial equality. And while the abolition of slavery was one of the two great results of the Civil War—the other being preservation of one nation indivisible—not many Union soldiers claimed to fight *primarily* for that purpose.

Four decades ago Bell Wiley wrote that scarcely one in ten Union soldiers "had any real interest in emancipation per se."[26] If by "per se" Wiley meant "in and of itself alone," one in ten may even be an exaggeration. Rare indeed were two soldiers, one from Wisconsin and the other from Maine, whose letters home contained such sentiments as: "I have no heart in this war if the slaves cannot go free. . . . [Our cause is] nobler even than the Revolution for they fought for their own freedom, while we fight for that of another race. . . . If the doom of slavery is not sealed by the war I shall curse the day I entered the Army or lifted a finger in the preservation of the Union."[27]

But if "emancipation per se" meant a perception that the abolition of slavery was inseparably linked to the goal of preserving the Union, then almost three in ten Union soldiers took this position during the first year and a half of the war, and many more were eventually converted to it. In November, 1861, a Massachusetts officer and Harvard graduate declared that "slavery has brought death into our own house-holds already in its wicked revolt against the government. . . . There is but one way, and that is emancipation; either that or we must succumb and divide." A stonemason who served as a private in another Massachusetts regiment considered "the object of our government as one worth dying to attain—the maintenance of our free institutions which must of *necessity* result in the freedom of every human being over whom the stars and stripes wave." Or as a twenty-year-old farm boy in the 1st Minnesota Infantry put it more succinctly in December, 1861: "The war will never end until we end slavery."[28]

But this was far from a universal opinion among Union soldiers. At times during the first two years of the war, for every soldier who held this opinion another expressed the opposite conviction: that emancipation was an unconstitutional and illegitimate war aim. Whereas a tacit consensus united Confederate soldiers in support of "southern institutions," including slavery, a bitter and explicit disagreement about emancipation divided northern soldiers. For six months during the winter and spring of 1862–1863, this question seriously sapped Union army morale. But unlike Confederate opinion on slavery, which remained relatively constant until the final months of the war, Union opinion was in a state of flux. It moved by fits and starts toward an eventual majority in favor of abolishing slavery as the only way to win the war and preserve the Union.

During the war's first year, the slavery issue seldom came up in the letters of most northern soldiers, for at this time the official war aim was only restoration of the Union. Nevertheless, during that year some soldiers predicted that the war must also become a fight to abolish slavery. A young school-teacher who enlisted in the 5th Wisconsin declared in August, 1861, that "I have been talking all my life for the cause of liberty but now the time is nigh at hand when I shall have a chance to aid by deed this cause." A farmer's son from Connecticut dropped out of Yale after his sophomore year in 1861 and enlisted in a cavalry regiment, as he explained to his mother, to fight "for Liberty, for the slave and the white man alike. . . . I have turned out to be a right out and out Abolitionist. The guaranties of the Constitution to Slavery, I claim, have been, one and all forfeited by the rebel slave owners." In July, 1861, a Union naval officer asserted that there would never "be peace between the two sections until slavery is so completely scotched [that] . . . we can see plainly in the future free labour to the gulph. . . . I think myself the Southerners are fighting against fate or human progress." [29] What is remarkable about this last quotation is that it came not from a Yankee fanatic but from Percival Drayton, a native of South Carolina and scion of a prominent planter family, whose brother Thomas Drayton became a Confederate general.

Experience in the South reinforced the convictions of most antislavery soldiers. After talking with a slave woman in Virginia who described the brutal whipping of her husband in a matter-of-fact way, a private in the crack 83d Pennsylvania wrote in January, 1862: "I thought I hated slavery as much as possible before I came here, but here, where I can see some of its workings, I am more than ever convinced of the cruelty and inhumanity of the system." More typical than such humanitarian concerns, however, was a contempt for southern ignorance and backwardness, which many Yankee soldiers attributed to slavery. An Ohio farmer's son who marched through Tennessee remarked on "how far behind the North they are in improvements of every kind. . . . The institution of slavery is as much a curse to the whites as the blacks and kills industry and improvements of every kind. Slavery has deadened all enterprise and prosperity. School houses are a rare sight." [30]

As northern armies penetrated into the South they became agents of emancipation by their mere presence. Slaves flocked to Union camps everywhere. Attempts by their masters to reclaim these fugitives turned soldiers previously indifferent toward slavery into practical abolitionists. Many letters tell of soldiers hiding fugitives in camp and laughing at the impotent rage of owners who went home empty-handed. Officers sometimes winked at this activity despite orders to the contrary. From Tennessee a Wisconsin soldier wrote home in March, 1862, that "whe have got lots of contraband negroes in our regt now and there is no less than two negro hunters in camp every day hunting for negroes Our colonel tells them if they can get them out of the lines they can have them but that is the trouble a negro hunter finds himself in a hot bed when he gets into the Regt they [throw] them out in a hurry." [31]

The attitudes of a good many soldiers on this matter were more pragmatic than altruistic. "I don't care a damn for the darkies," wrote an Illinois lieutenant, but "I couldn't help to send a runaway nigger back. I'm blamed if I could. I honestly believe that this army has taken 500 niggers away with them." In fact, "I have 11 negroes in my company now. They do every particle of the dirty work. Two women among them do the washing for the company." Another Illinois soldier, an infantry sergeant, wrote from Corinth, Mississippi, in 1862 that "every regt has nigger teamsters and cooks which puts that many more men back in the ranks. . . . It will make a difference in the regt of not less than 75 men that will carry guns that did not before we got niggers." [32]

By the summer of 1862, antislavery principle and pragmatism fused into a growing commitment to emancipation as both a means and an end of Union victory. This development represented a significant hardening of northern attitudes toward "traitors," whose rights of property—especially property in slaves—were entitled to little respect. "We have been . . . playing with *Traitors* long enough" was a typical phrase in soldiers' letters. "This thing of guarding rebels property has about 'played out.' . . . We have guarded their homes and property long enough, now is the time for action. . . . The only way to put down this rebellion is to hurt the instigators and abettors of it. Slavery must be cleaned out. . . . The time has come to march through this nest of vipers with fire and sword, to liberate every slave." [33]

Officials in Washington came to the same conclusion. In July, 1862, Congress passed the second confiscation act and Lincoln made his momentous decision to issue an emancipation proclamation. It would not become public for two months, but meanwhile the work of practical emancipation went on. "That bill to confiscate the rebel property is just what we want," wrote a Rhode Island sergeant. "If a rebels property gits eney favers from eney of our Soldiers you can call me a poore judge." The colonel of the 5th Minnesota wrote from northern Alabama in September, 1862, that "I am doing quite a business in the confiscation of slave property. . . . It certainly makes the rebels wince to see their 'niggers' taken off which is a source of private satisfaction to me. . . . Crippling the institution of slavery is . . . striking a blow at the heart of the rebellion." [34]

But a good many Union soldiers disagreed. A backlash of antiemancipation sentiment began to surface in the letters of a number of them in 1862. This sentiment brewed up from a mixture of racism, conservatism, and partisan politics. The experiences and observations in the South that made some soldiers more antislavery made others more antiblack. "No one who has ever seen the nigger in all his glory on the southern plantations will ever vote for emancipation," wrote an Indiana private. "If emancipation is to be the policy of this war . . . I do not care how quick the country goes to pot." An abolitionist clergyman's son in the 12th Maine wrote home from Louisiana in the summer of 1862 that "I do not want to hear any more about negroes when I get home. . . . I have got sick and tired of them . . . and I shall hereafter let abolition alone. . . . They are a set of thieves . . . and the boys here hate them worse than they do secesh." An artillery major from New York, a Democrat like so many officers in the Army of the Potomac under McClellan, wrote that if Lincoln caved in to "these 'black Republicans'" and made it "an abolition war[,] . . . I for one shall be sorry that I ever lent a hand to it. . . . This war [must be] for the preservation of the Union, the putting down of armed rebellion, and for that purpose only."[35]

This major spoke for a substantial number of Union soldiers. After all, at least two-fifths of them were Democrats and another tenth came from border states. Their resistance to any notion of turning the war for Union into a war against slavery was one reason for Lincoln's hesitancy to do just that. The cause of Union united northern soldiers; the cause of emancipation divided them. Letters and diaries mention vigorous campfire arguments about slavery. A Massachusetts sergeant made the following entry in his diary for February 4, 1863: "Had a jaw on slavery in the evening, & Jim did n't agree with the rest of us, & so he got mad." At about the same time an Indiana corporal wrote in his diary: "At night got into an argument, with a man that believed Slavery is right.—Had a warm time." A New York lieutenant wrote to his sister in January, 1863, that in his officers' mess "we have had several pretty spirited, I may call them *hot*, controversies about slavery, the Emancipation Edict and kindred subjects."[36]

It was no accident that these heated discussions took place

during the winter of 1862–1863. The Emancipation Proclamation provoked a new level of consciousness about the relationship of slavery to the war. Soldiers who had advocated an antislavery war from the beginning naturally welcomed the proclamation. As a captain in the 46th Pennsylvania put it, Lincoln's action made the war no longer merely a contest "between North & South; but a contest between human rights and human liberty on one side and eternal bondage on the other." A Minnesota corporal wrote approvingly to his wife: "Abraham 'has gone and done it' at last. Yesterday will be a day hallowed in the hearts of millions of the people of these United States, & also by the friends of liberty and humanity the *world* over."[37] In a letter to his fiancée an Illinois cavalry sergeant quoted with admiration the peroration of Lincoln's message to Congress in December, 1862: "In *giving* freedom to the *slave,* we *assure* freedom to the free." Several soldiers rang changes on the theme expressed by a New York private: "Thank God . . . the contest is now between Slavery & freedom, & every honest man knows what he is fighting for."[38]

These were the idealists. The pragmatists weighed in with equally forceful, if less elegant, expressions. "I am no abolitionist," wrote an enlisted man in the 55th Ohio, "in fact despise the word," but "as long as slavery exists . . . there will be no permanent peace for America. . . . Hence I am in favor of killing slavery." An Indiana sergeant told his wife that while he had no use for free blacks, he approved the Emancipation Proclamation "if it will only bring the war to an end any sooner I am like the fellow that got his house burned by the guerrillas he was in for emancipation subjugation extermination and hell and damnation. We are in war and anything to beat the South."[39] As for those who howl that we are now "fighting for the nigger," rather than for Union, wrote a forty-year-old Ohio private to his wife, "if they are such fools as not to be able to see the difference between the means employed, and the end in view, let them remain blind."[40]

But plenty of soldiers believed that the proclamation *had* changed the purpose of the war. They professed to feel betrayed. They were willing to risk their lives for Union, they said, but not for black freedom. The proclamation intensified a morale crisis in Union armies during the winter of 1862–1863, especially in the Army of the Potomac. The removal of McClellan from command, the disaster at Fredericksburg, and the fiasco of the Mud March had caused morale in that army to plunge to an all-time low. Things were little better in Grant's army on the Mississippi, where the first attempts against Vicksburg had come to grief.

Desertion rates in both armies rose alarmingly. Many soldiers blamed the Emancipation Proclamation. The "men are much dissatisfied" with it, reported a New York captain, "and say that it has turned into a 'nigger war' and all are anxious to return to their homes for it was to preserve the Union that they volunteered." Enlisted men confirmed this observation with a blizzard of bitter comments in letters home. "I am the Boy that Can fight for my Country," wrote an Illinois private, "but not for the Negros."[41] A private in the 66th Indiana wrote from Mississippi in February, 1863, that he and his messmates "will not fite to free the niger . . . there is a Regment her that say they will never fite untill the proclamation is with drawn there is four of the Capt[ains] in our Regt sent in there Resingnations and one of the Liutenants there was nine in Comp. G tride to desert." At the end of 1862 another Illinois soldier with a wife and children reflected on the "cost of freeing the Black Devils. No less than 300,000 of our own free white citizens have already been sacrificed to free the small mite that have got their freedom. . . . I consider the life & Happiness of my family of more value than any Nigger."[42]

How widespread were such attitudes? How dangerous were they to the morale and cohesion of Union armies? The answers are difficult to quantify precisely. For a time during the winter of 1862–1863, antiemancipation expressions seemed to outnumber those on the other side. And morale certainly declined—although defeatism and lack of faith in Union leaders may have had more to do with this than the Emancipation Proclamation. In any case, the decline of morale proved short-lived, for the Union armies did not fall apart and soon won some of their most decisive victories of the war. And of the soldiers in my sample who expressed a clear opinion about emancipation as a war aim at any time through the spring of 1863, two and one-half times as many favored it as opposed it: 36 percent to 14 percent. If we apportion those who did not comment on the subject evenly between the two sides, the picture would conform with the results of a poll in March, 1863, in the 15th Iowa, a fairly typical regiment. Half of the men endorsed the Emancipation Proclamation, a quarter opposed it, and the other quarter did not register an opinion.[43]

These figures undoubtedly understate antiemancipation sentiment, for the regiment's colonel was a strong supporter of the proclamation and the poll was an open one. The two-and-one-half-to-one majority for emancipation in my sample also probably overstates the margin in the army as a whole, because proemancipation sentiment was strongest among those groups overrepresented in the sample—officers, and men from professional and white-collar occupations—and underrepresents the less educated soldiers from blue-collar and immigrant backgrounds among whom antiblack and antiemancipation attitudes were strongest.

Nevertheless, the evidence indicates that proemancipation convictions did predominate among the leaders and fighting soldiers of the Union army. And that prevalence increased after the low point of early 1863 as a good many antieman-cipation soldiers changed their minds. Two factors played a part in their conversion. The first was a dangerous rise of copperheadism on the home front during the first half of 1863. Peace Democrats zeroed in on the Emancipation Proc-lamation in their denunciations of Lincoln's unconstitutional war and their demands for a negotiated peace. This produced an anticopperhead backlash among Union soldiers, including many Democrats, that catapulted some of them clear into the Lincoln camp on emancipation. This pilgrimage can be traced in the letters of two Ohio soldiers, one a nineteen-year-old private and the other a thirty-four-year-old colonel.

For three months after the Emancipation Proclamation, Private Chauncey Welton of the 103d Ohio damned it up and down and backward and forward in letters to his family, staunch Democrats all. "I enlisted to fight for and vindicate the supremacy of the constitution," he wrote, but "we did not enlist to fight for the negro and I can tell you that *we never shall* . . . sacrafise [our] lives for the liberty of a miserable black race of beings." But then he began to change his tune, especially after Clement L. Vallandigham was nominated for governor of Ohio on an antiwar platform, which "fell like a thunderbolt on this regiment," reported Welton. By June, 1863, he had become converted to the idea that abolition of slavery was "a means of haistening the speedy Restoration of the union and the termination of the war." This letter fell like a thunderbolt on his father, who regarded it as heresy. But young Welton became a Republican, and by early 1865 he sounded just like an abolitionist when he wrote in joyful an-ticipation of a restored nation "*free free free* yes free from that blighting curs *Slavery* the cause of four years of Bloody Warfare."[44]

As colonel of the 67th Ohio, Marcus Spiegel was the highest-ranking officer of the Jewish faith in the Civil War.

As a Democrat he denounced the Emancipation Proclamation, writing to his wife in January, 1863: "I am sick of the war. . . . I do not fight or want to fight for Lincoln's Negro proclamation one day longer." But when his men began to say the same thing, repeating what they had heard from home or read in Democratic newspapers, Spiegel grew alarmed. "Stand by the government right or wrong," he told his regiment. By April, 1863, he had repudiated the Democratic party; by January, 1864, a few months before he was killed in the Red River campaign, he wrote his wife from Plaquemines Parish, Louisiana, that "since I [came] here I have learned and seen more of what the horrors of Slavery was than I ever knew before. . . . I am [in] favor of doing away with the . . . accursed institution. . . . I am [now] a strong abolitionist."[45]

The second factor that converted many soldiers to support of emancipation was a growing conviction that it really did hurt the enemy and help their own side. In this respect the contribution of black soldiers—whose enlistment was a corollary of the emancipation policy—did much to change the minds of previously hostile white soldiers. A junior officer in the 86th Indiana reported in March, 1863, that men who two months earlier had damned the "*abolition war*" and threatened to desert now favored both emancipation and black soldiers. "We use all other kinds of rebel property," he wrote, "and they see no reason why we should not use negroes. Every negro we get strengthens us and weakens the rebels. The soldiers now say if there can be negroes enough raised to conquer the rebels let them do it." An antebellum Douglas Democrat from Illinois wrote his wife in 1863 that his regiment had confiscated horses and liberated hundreds of slaves in middle Tennessee. "Now what do you think of your husband degenerating from a conservative young Democrat to a horse stealer and 'nigger thief'?" he asked her playfully.

"So long as [my] flag is confronted by the hostile guns of slavery . . . I am as confirmed an abolitionist as ever was pelted with stale eggs."[46]

Not all antiabolitionist soldiers experienced such a conversion. An Indiana private decided against reenlisting for another three-year hitch because the war had become a crusade "to Free the Nigars . . . and I do not propose to fight any more in such a cause." A private in the 6th Kentucky complained in the spring of 1864 that "this is nothing but an abolition war. . . . I am a strait out Union and Constitution man I am not for freeing the negroes." His brother in the same regiment agreed and added a wish that "old abe lincoln . . . had to sleep with a negro evry night as long as he lives and kiss ones ass twice a day."[47]

But this was a distinctly minority view among Union soldiers by 1864. When Lincoln ran for reelection that year on a platform pledging a constitutional amendment to abolish slavery, he received nearly 80 percent of the soldier vote— a pretty fair indication of army sentiment on slavery by that time. "It is astonishing how things has changed in reference to freeing the Negros," wrote a soldier from Lincoln's state, a farmer by trade. "It allwais has been plane to me that this rase must be freed befor god would recognise us . . . we bost of liberty and we Should not be Selfish in it as god gives us liberty we Should try to impart it to others. . . . thank god the chanes will Soon be bursted . . . now I belive we are on gods side . . . now I can fight with a good heart." A Michigan sergeant in his forties, also a farmer, wrote his wife from Georgia in the spring of 1864 that "the more I learn of the cursed institution of Slavery, the more I feel willing to endure, for its final destruction. . . . After this war is over, this whole country will undergo a change for the better . . . abolishing slavery will dignify labor; that fact of itself will revolutionize everything."[48] He never experienced disappointment with this vision of the future; an enemy sharpshooter ended his life near Atlanta in August, 1864.

Had the Michigan sergeant lived to witness the North's retreat from Reconstruction in the 1870s and the South's disfranchisement and formalized segregation of blacks in the 1890s, he might have wondered whether the abolition of slavery had revolutionized everything after all. By the 1890s the road to reunion between men who wore the blue and gray had paved over the issues of slavery and equal rights for freed slaves. Middle-aged veterans in the Grand Army of the Republic and the United Confederate Veterans held joint encampments at which they reminisced about the glorious deeds of their youth. Many of them reached a tacit consensus, which some voiced openly: Confederate soldiers had not fought for slavery; Union soldiers had not fought for its abolition. It had been a tragic war of brothers whose issues were best forgotten in the interests of family reconciliation. In the popular romanticization of the Civil War, the issue of slavery became almost as invisible as black Union veterans at a reunion encampment. Somehow the Civil War became a heroic contest, a sort of grand, if deadly, football game without ideological cause or purpose.

Some veterans, however, dissented from the tendency to blur the issues of the war, especially slavery. Their most eloquent spokesman was Oliver Wendell Holmes, Jr. Twenty years after he had described the Union cause as "the Christian crusade of the 19th century," Holmes declared in a Memorial Day address to other veterans in 1884 that "in our youth our hearts were touched with fire. It was given to us to learn at the outset that life is a profound and passionate thing."[49] Like Holmes, many Civil War soldiers felt a profound and passionate commitment to the ideological purposes for which they fought. If some of them later forgot this, there is no better way to recover what motivated them from 1861 to 1865 than to read their letters and diaries written in the immediacy of experience. Only then can we truly understand what they fought for.

NOTES

INTRODUCTION

1. William Faulkner, *Sartoris* (New York, 1929), 227; Fred A. Bailey, *Class and Tennessee's Confederate Generation* (Chapel Hill, 1987), 78; *New Yorker,* May 18, 1992, p. 31.

2. Gerald F. Linderman, *Embattled Courage: The Experience of Combat in the American Civil War* (New York, 1987), 80; Reid Mitchell, *Civil War Soldiers: Their Expectations and Their Experiences* (New York, 1988), 18. In a new study that appeared as this book went to press, Mitchell makes an effective case for the power of patriotism and ideological commitment, mediated through the institutions of home and community, in motivating Union soldiers to fight. Reid Mitchell, *The Vacant Chair: The Northern Soldier Leaves Home* (New York, 1993).

3. Bell Irvin Wiley, *The Life of Johnny Reb: The Common Soldier of the Confederacy* (Indianapolis, 1943), 309; Wiley, *The Life of Billy Yank: The Common Soldier of the Union* (Indianapolis, 1952), 39–40.

4. Samuel A. Stouffer *et al., The American Soldier* (4 vols.; Princeton, 1949), esp. Vol. II, *Combat and Its Aftermath;* Samuel L. A. Marshall, *Men Against Fire* (New York, 1947), 160–61.

5. Stouffer *et al., American Soldier,* II, 169.

6. Elmar Dinter, *Hero or Coward: Pressures Facing the Soldier in Battle,* trans. Tricia Hughes (London, 1985), 177; Stouffer *et al., American Soldier,* II, 150.

7. "Robert A. Moore: The Diary of a Confederate Private," ed. James W. Silver, *Louisiana Historical Quarterly,* XXXIX (1956), entry of January 28, 1862, p. 312; William J. Mims to his wife, September 22, 1864, in "Letters of Major W. J. Mims, C.S.A.," *Alabama Historical Quarterly,* III (1941), 223.

8. Samuel J. Harrison Diary, September 10, 12, 13, October 15, 1864, in Harrison Papers, OHS.

9. Mary Ann Anderson, ed., *The Civil War Diary of Allen Morgan Geer* (Denver, 1977), entries of November 30, December 24, 31, November 1, 1863, pp. 142, 147, 149, 136.

10. Thomas Kilby Smith to Eliza Smith, February 4, 1863, in Smith Papers, HEH; Nelson Chapin to his wife, March 6, 1864, in Chapin Papers, CWTI Collection, USAMHI; Ulysses S. Grant, *Personal Memoirs of U. S. Grant* (2 vols.; New York, 1885), II, 531.

11. Chapin to wife, March 6, 1864, in Chapin Papers; Henry M. Howell to Emily Howell, December 7, 1864, in *This Regiment of Heroes: A Compilation of Primary Materials Pertaining to the 124th New York State Volunteers,* ed. Charles J. Larocca (Montgomery, N.Y., 1991), 230.

12. Roy P. Basler, ed., *The Collected Works of Abraham Lincoln* (9 vols.; New Brunswick, N.J., 1952–55), VII, 23; Dunbar Rowland, ed., *Jefferson Davis, Constitutionalist: His Letters, Papers, and Speeches* (10 vols.; Jackson, Miss., 1923), V, 202.

CHAPTER 1

1. Thomas Rowland to his mother, June 14, July 29, 1861, in "Letters of Major Thomas Rowland, C.S.A., from the Camps at Ashland and Richmond, Virginia, 1861," *William and Mary College Quarterly,* XXIV (1915–16), 148–49, 234; Rowland to his aunt, December 10, 1861, in "Letters of Major Thomas Rowland, C.S.A., from North Carolina, 1861 and 1862," *William and Mary College Quarterly,* XXV (1916–17), 80; Henry Orr to his sister, October 31, 1861, in *Campaigning with Parsons' Texas Cavalry Brigade, C.S.A.,* ed. John Q. Anderson (Hillsboro, Tex., 1967), 10.

2. Eugene Blackford to his mother, February 22, 1862, in Gordon-Blackford Papers, MDHS; "Civil War Journal of James E. Paton," ed. Mrs. Wade Hampton Whitley, *Register of the Kentucky Historical Society,* LXI (1963), entries of July 4, July 2, 1862, pp. 228, 220; John G. Barrett, ed., *Yankee Rebel: The Civil War Journal of Edmund DeWitt Patterson* (Chapel Hill, 1966), entry of July 4, 1863, p. 119.

3. William O. Fleming to Georgia Fleming, July 13, 1863, in Fleming Papers, SHC, UNC; William C. Proffit to Andrew J. Proffit, May 10, 1862, in Proffit Family Papers, *ibid.*

4. Nathaniel H. R. Dawson to Elodie Todd, June 8, 1861, in Dawson Papers, *ibid;* S. J. McLeroy to his wife, July 3, 1864, in John Cumming Papers, PLDU.

5. Noah Dixon Walker to his father, February 10, 1863, in Noah D.

Walker Papers, MDHS; George M. Lee to Jordan G. Taylor, August 26, 1861, in "A Collection of Louisiana Confederate Letters," ed. Frank E. Vandiver, *Louisiana Historical Quarterly,* XXVI (1943), 941; Joseph Mothershead Diary, June 13, 1862, in TSL.

6. William E. Coleman to his parents, January 19, 1862, in Coleman Letters, Civil War Collection, TSL; John N. Shealy to Eugenia Shealy, June 27, 1862, in Shealy Papers, HML, LSU.

7. Samuel F. Tenney to Alice Toomer, January 18, 1862, in "War Letters of S. F. Tenney, a Soldier of the Third Georgia Regiment," *Georgia Historical Quarterly,* LVII (1973), 280; Alexander S. Pendleton to William N. Pendleton, February 25, 1862, in "The Valley Campaign of 1862 as Revealed in Letters of Sandie Pendleton," ed. W. G. Bean, *Virginia Magazine of History and Biography,* LXXVIII (1970), 332.

8. Thomas J. Goree to Mary Frances Goree Kittrell, February 18, 1862, Goree to Robert D. Goree, December 18, 1864, in *The Thomas Jewett Goree Letters: The Civil War Correspondence,* ed. Langston James Goree (Bryan, Tex., 1981), 135, 238; Joseph C. Webb to Robina Norwood, September 19, 1863, in *Echoes of Happy Valley: Letters and Diaries of Family Life in the South and Civil War History,* ed. Thomas Felix Hickerson (Chapel Hill, 1962), 75.

9. Ernest Hemingway, *A Farewell to Arms* (New York, 1929), 191, 196; Paul Fussell, *The Great War and Modern Memory* (New York, 1975), 21–22.

10. Edward W. Cade to his wife, January 30, July 9, November 19, 1863, in *A Texas Surgeon in the C.S.A.,* ed. John Q. Anderson (Tuscaloosa, 1957), 33, 67–68, 81.

11. John W. Reese to his wife, May 26, 1863, in Reese Papers, PLDU; James C. Zimmerman to Adeline Zimmerman, August 5, 1863, in Zimmerman Papers, *ibid.*

12. "The Diary of H. C. Medford, Confederate Soldier, 1864," ed. Rebecca W. Smith and Marion Mullins, *Southwestern Historical Quarterly,* XXXIV (1930), entries of April 4, 8, 1864, pp. 211, 220; Hannibal Paine to Miss Jennie, January 12, 1863, Hannibal Paine to F. J. Paine, August 30, 1861, both in Paine Papers, TSL.

13. George Knox Miller to Celestine McCann, June 10, 1861, in Miller Papers, SHC, UNC; George Loyall Gordon to Mary Gordon, July 3, 1861, June 17, 1862, in Gordon Papers, SHC, UNC.

14. Anthony Kellett, *Combat Motivation: The Behavior of Soldiers in Battle* (Boston, 1982), 175–76.

15. Olney Andrus to Mary Andrus, November 9, 1862, in *The Civil War Letters of Sergeant Olney Andrus*, ed. Fred A. Shannon (Urbana, Ill., 1947), 25—26; Frederick Bartleson to Kate Bartleson, February 26, 1864, in *The Brothers' War*, ed. Annette Tapert (New York, 1988), 187.

16. W. M. Clark to his wife, August 26, 1861, in "A Confederate Officer Visits Richmond," ed. Sam L. Clark, *Tennessee Historical Quarterly*, XI (1952), 91; James K. Edmondson to Emma Edmondson, March 13, 1862, in *My Dear Emma: War Letters of Col. James K. Edmondson, 1861–1865*, ed. Charles S. Turner (Verona, Va., 1978), 86; William Fisher Plane to Helen Plane, June 1, 1861, in "Letters of William Fisher Plane, C.S.A., to His Wife," ed. S. Joseph Lewis, Jr., *Georgia Historical Quarterly*, XLVIII (1964), 217; Hannibal Paine to Miss Virginia, July 26, 1861, in Paine Papers, TSL; "The Justness of Our Cause: The Civil War Diaries of William W. Stringfield," ed. Vernon H. Crow, *East Tennessee Historical Publications*, LVI (1984), entry of April 19, 1861, p. 72; John Q. Winfield to Sallie Winfield, September 2, 1861, in Winfield Papers, SHC, UNC; Richard M. Saffell to Mrs. John Bogle, November 24, 1861, in Saffell letters (in private possession, cited courtesy of Hal Saffell).

17. Cadwalader J. Iredell to Mattie Iredell, March 18, 1865, in Iredell Papers, SHC, UNC; Thomas H. Colman to parents, n.d. [April, 1862], in Colman-Hayter Papers, State Historical Society of Missouri, Columbia.

18. W. W. Jackson to Mary Jewel, January 18, 1864, in Jewel Family Papers, State Historical Society of Missouri, Columbia; James West Smith, "A Confederate Soldier's Diary: Vicksburg in 1863," *Southwest Review*, XXVIII (1943), entries of June 2, 15, 1863, pp. 304, 312; "Civil War Journal of James E. Paton," ed. Mrs. Wade Hampton Whitley, *Register of the Kentucky Historical Society*, LXI (1963), entry of July 2, 1862, p. 220; Brother Willie to Mrs. E. P. Alexander, February 2, 1864, in E. P. Alexander Papers, SHC, UNC.

19. Dorsey Pender to Fanny Pender, June 6, 1862, in *The General to His Lady*, ed. Warren W. Hassler (Chapel Hill, 1966), 152.

20. John Collins to Mary Collins, April 8, 1862, in Collins Papers, VHS; Edward M. Burrus to his mother, June 14, 1862, in Burrus Family Papers, HML, LSU; Harry Lewis to his mother, August 9, 1862, in Harry Lewis Papers, SHC, UNC.

21. Benjamin F. Batchelor to Julia Batchelor, December 19, 1861, in *Batchelor-Turner Letters, 1861–1864, Written by Two of Terry's Texas Rangers*, ed. Helen J. H. Rugeley (Austin, 1961), 3; Elijah Petty to his wife,

September 11, 1862, May 22, 1863, Petty to his daughter, May 10, 1863, all in *Journey to Pleasant Hill: The Civil War Letters of Captain Elijah P. Petty*, ed. Norman D. Brown (San Antonio, 1982), 78–79, 223, 215.

22. Richard Henry Watkins to Mary Watkins, April 18, 1862, in Watkins Papers, VHS; Edwin H. Fay to Sarah Fay, September 19, June 27, July 10, 1863, in *"This Infernal War": The Confederate Letters of Sgt. Edwin H. Fay*, ed. Bell Irvin Wiley (Austin, 1958), 329, 286–87, 292.

23. James H. Langhorne to John Langhorne, December 15, 1861, in Langhorne Papers, VHS; H. Christopher Kendrick to his father, June 6, 1863, and n.d. [1863], in Kendrick Papers, SHC, UNC; Eugene Blackford to Mary L. Minor, n.d. [early September, 1864], in Gordon-Blackford Papers.

24. Osmun Latrobe Diary, December 16, 1862, in MDHS; Thomas H. Colman to parents, October 5, 1863, in Colman-Hayter Papers.

25. Edward M. Burrus to parents, n.d. [late September, 1862], in Burrus Papers; John O. Collins to his wife, August 17, 1863, in Collins Papers, VHS.

26. Eldred Simkins to Eliza Trescott, August 8, September 14, 17, 1864, in Simkins Papers, HEH.

27. Thomas J. Key Diary, August 8, 29, 1864, February 5, 1865, in *Two Soldiers: The Campaign Diaries of Thomas J. Key, C.S.A., and Robert J. Campbell, U.S.A.*, ed. Wirt Armistead Cate (Chapel Hill, 1938), 111, 123, 187; "War Diary of Captain Robert Emory Park, Twelfth Alabama Regiment," *Southern Historical Society Papers*, II (1876), entry of December 24, 1864, p. 237; Barrett, ed., *Yankee Rebel*, entry of March 26, 1865, pp. 205–206.

28. Neal F. Heendy to Bryant Wright, February 14, 1864, in Wright Papers, PLDU; John Weaton to Laura, January 19, 1864, in Lewis Leigh Collection, USAMHI; Sydney S. Champion to his wife, June 1, 1864, in Champion Papers, PLDU.

29. "War Diary of Captain Robert Emory Park," December 24, 1864, p. 237.

CHAPTER 2

1. John B. Jones, *A Rebel War Clerk's Diary*, ed. Earl Schenck Miers (New York, 1958), entry of March 29, 1863, p. 181.

2. William S. Stewart to his parents, September 6, July 18, 1861, in "William S. Stewart Letters, Jan. 13, 1861, to Dec. 4, 1862," ed. Harvey

L. Carter and Norma L. Peterson, *Missouri Historical Review*, LXI (1966–67), 224, 291; Delos Lake to Calvin Lake, September 20, 1863, in Lake Papers, HEH.

3. Robert McAllister to Ellen McAllister, December 24, 27, 1861, in *The Civil War Letters of General Robert McAllister*, ed. James I. Robertson, Jr. (New Brunswick, N.J., 1965), 106, 107; Joseph Fardell to his parents, July 11, 1863, in Fardell Papers, Missouri Historical Society, St. Louis.

4. Leander Stem to Amanda Stem, December 15, 1862, in "Stand by the Colors: The Civil War Letters of Leander Stem," ed. John T. Hubbell, *Register of the Kentucky Historical Society*, LXXIII (1975), 408; Philo H. Gallup to John S. Gallup, May 8, 1861, in "The Second Michigan Volunteer Infantry Joins the Army of the Potomac: Letters of Philo H. Gallup," ed. Chester M. Destler, *Michigan History*, XLI (1957), 388.

5. Thomas T. Taylor to Antoinette Taylor, May 23, June 18, 1861, February 25, June 7, 1862, in Taylor Papers, OHS; Ephraim S. Holloway to Margaret Holloway, June 14, July 11, 1862, March 30, 1864, in Holloway Papers, *ibid;* Josiah Chaney to Melissa Chaney, October 3, 1862, in Chaney Papers, MNHS.

6. Samuel McIlvaine to "Mother and Friends," September 29, 1862, in *By the Dim and Flaring Lamps: The Civil War Diaries of Samuel McIlvaine*, ed. Clayton E. Cramer (New York, 1990), 147.

7. Josiah Perry to Phebe Perry, October 3, 1862, in Perry Papers, ISHL; Robert Goodyear to Sarah Goodyear, February 14, 1863, in Goodyear Letters, USAMHI.

8. Robert T. McMahan Diary, entry of September 5, 1863, in State Historical Society of Missouri, Columbia; Robert McAllister to Ellen McAllister, in *Civil War Letters of General Robert McAllister*, ed. Robertson, 608.

9. George H. Cadman to Esther Cadman, March 6, 1864, in Cadman Papers, SHC, UNC.

10. Peter Welsh to Mary Welsh, February 3, 1863, Peter Welsh to Patrick Prendergast, June 1, 1863, both in *Irish Green and Union Blue: The Civil War Letters of Peter Welsh*, ed. Laurence Frederick Kohl and Margaret Cosse Richard (New York, 1986), 65–66, 102.

11. Roy P. Basler, ed., *The Collected Works of Abraham Lincoln* (9 vols.; New Brunswick, N.J., 1952–55), IV, 268. For an acute analysis of this theme, see Phillip S. Paludan, "The American Civil War Considered as

a Crisis in Law and Order," *American Historical Review,* LXXVII (1972), 1013–1034.

12. Dan G. Porter to Maria Lewis, July 24, 1862, in "The Civil War Letters of Captain Andrew Lewis and His Daughter," ed. Michael Barton, *Western Pennsylvania Magazine of History,* LX (1977), 389; Delos Van Deusen to Henrietta Van Deusen, December 23, 1862, in Van Deusen Papers, HEH; John Beatty, *Memoirs of a Volunteer, 1861–1865* (New York, 1946), Diary entry of July 3, 1862, p. 115.

13. Henry S. Gansevoort to his father, August 4, 1861, in *Memorial of Henry Sanford Gansevoort,* ed. John D. Hoadley (Boston, 1875), 95; Samuel R. Curtis to his wife, March 4, 1861, in " 'The Irrepressible Conflict of 1861': The Letters of Samuel Ryan Curtis," *Annals of Iowa,* 3d Series, XXIV (1942–43), 37.

14. George W. Beidelman to his father, August 5, 1862, in *The Civil War Letters of George Washington Beidelman,* ed. Catherine H. Vanderslice (New York, 1978), 73; Samuel Evans to his father, September 13, 1863, in Evans Family Papers, OHS. I am indebted to Professor Robert Engs of the University of Pennsylvania for calling the Evans collection to my attention.

15. William Henry Cooley to his parents, June 2, 1861, in Cooley Papers, SHC, UNC; Lyman G. Bennett Diary, October 5, 1861, in State Historical Society of Missouri, Columbia; Joseph H. Griner to Sophia Griner, January 3, 1863, in Daniel H. Woodward, "The Civil War of a Pennsylvania Trooper," *Pennsylvania Magazine of History and Biography,* LXXXVII (1963), 51.

16. William H. Wykoff to Richard Parry, May 27, 1863, in Wykoff letters (in private possession, cited courtesy of J. M. Dobie); Nelson Chapin to his wife, October 19, 1863, in Chapin Papers, CWTI Collection, USAMHI.

17. Edgar Ketcham to his mother, November 18, 1862, May 12, 1863, Edgar Ketcham to John Ketcham, January 11, 1863, John Ketcham to his mother, July 8, 1863, all in *The Fighting Quakers: A True Story of the War for Our Union,* ed. A. J. H. Duganne (New York, 1866), 38–39, 61–62, 51, 80.

18. James Bell to Augusta Hallock, January 14, 1863, in Bell Collection, HEH; Edward Wightman to Fred Wightman, January 3, 1863, in *From Antietam to Fort Fisher: The Civil War Letters of Edward King Wightman, 1862–1865* (Rutherford, N.J., 1983), 99.

19. Robert Gooding to his brother, April 13, December 14, 1862, in

Gooding Papers, State Historical Society of Missouri, Columbia; Henry H. Perry to his mother, August 14, 1864, in Perry Papers (in private possession, cited courtesy of Henry Perry).

20. Louis A. Hammontree to James Hammontree, June 6, 1864, in "The Hammontrees Fight the Civil War: Letters from the Fifth East Tennessee Infantry," ed. Lewis A. Lawson, *Lincoln Herald*, LXXVIII (1976), 118; John D. Mitchell to Absalom B. Barner, June 6, 1862, in "Selected Civil War Letters from Collection of Dr. William F. Hawn, Louisville, Kentucky," *Register of the Kentucky Historical Society*, LXXI (1973), 298.

21. Thomas T. Taylor to Antoinette Taylor, October 16, 1861, in Taylor Papers, OHS; Philander Draper to Edwin Draper, July 12, 1861, in Draper-McClurg Papers, State Historical Society of Missouri, Columbia; William and Henry Crawford to "Dear Friends," August 5, 1864, in Crawford Letters, State Historical Society of Missouri.

22. Samuel Cormany Diary, September 13, 1862, in *The Cormany Diaries: A Northern Family in the Civil War*, ed. James C. Mohr (Pittsburgh, 1982), 230; William B. Baker to Fannie Baker, July 7, 1863, in Baker Papers, SHC, UNC.

23. Augustus Barr to his wife, September 18, 1862, in John Arick Papers, HRT Collection, USAMHI; Judson L. Austin to Sarah Austin, December 18, August 26, 1863, in Austin Papers (in private possession, cited courtesy of Dave Holmquist).

24. Delavan Arnold to his mother, April 21, 1862, in *A Kalamazoo Volunteer in the Civil War*, ed. Thomas O. McConnell (Kalamazoo, Mich., 1962), 22; Daniel Warden to his aunt, March 17, 1862, in Warden Letters, USAMHI.

25. Squire Tuttle to parents, June 19, 1864, Tuttle to his brother and sister, June 27, 1864, both in Tuttle Papers, USAMHI.

26. John Brobst to Mary Englesby, May 20, July 11, 1864, in *Well, Mary: Civil War Letters of a Wisconsin Volunteer*, ed. Margaret B. Roth (Madison, Wisc., 1960), 56—57, 75.

27. Charles Wills to his sister, September 17, 1861, in *Army Life of an Illinois Soldier: Letters and Diary of the Late Charles Wills* (Washington, D.C., 1906), 32; Stephen Weld to his mother, June 10, 1863, in *War Diary and Letters of Stephen Minot Weld, 1861–1865*, ed. Stephen M. Weld (Boston, 1979), 212–13; John Beatty to Laura Beatty, July 30, 1864, in Beatty Papers, MNHS.

28. Ira Payne to his parents, March 1, 1863, in Payne Papers, ISHL.

29. Isaac Jackson to Moses and Phebe Jackson, July 13, 1863, in

"Some of the Boys . . . ": The Civil War Letters of Isaac Jackson, 1862–1865 (Carbondale, Ill., 1960), 111–12; George M. Wise to John Wise, March 13, 1865, in "Civil War Letters of George M. Wise," ed. Wilfred W. Black, *Ohio Historical Quarterly,* LXVI (1957), 193.

30. Gerald F. Linderman, *Embattled Courage: The Experience of Combat in the American Civil War* (New York, 1987), 240; Leif Torkelsen, "Forged in Battle: The Evolution of Small Unit Cohesion in the Union Volunteer Infantry Regiments, 1861–1865" (Senior thesis, Princeton University, 1991), 5.

31. Josiah M. Favill, *Diary of a Young Officer* (Chicago, 1909), entry of January 1, 1864, p. 273; Henry Henney Diary, entries of October 15, 1864, September 21, 1863, Henry Henney to his sister, April 1, 1863, all in Henney Papers, CWTI Collection, USAMHI.

32. Oliver Wendell Holmes, Jr., to Charles Eliot Norton, April 17, 1864, in *Touched with Fire: Civil War Letters and Diary of Oliver Wendell Holmes, Jr., 1861–1865,* ed. Mark De Wolfe Howe (Cambridge, Mass., 1946), 122n; Alfred Lacey Hough to Mary Hough, October 28, 1863, March 13, 1864, in *Soldier in the West: The Civil War Letters of Alfred Lacey Hough,* ed. Robert G. Athearn (Philadelphia, 1957), 165, 178.

33. Bliss Morse to his mother, August 29, 1864, in *War Diaries and Letters of Bliss Morse,* ed. Loren J. Morse (Tahlequah, Okla., 1985) 150; Bliss Morse Diary, November 8, 1864, *ibid.,* 165; Wash Vosburgh to Ella, January 10, March 19, 1864, in Vosburgh Papers, Bentley Library, University of Michigan.

34. Edward Wightman to Fred Wightman, August 28, 1864, in *From Antietam to Fort Fisher,* 206; Edmund English to his mother, April 12, 1863, April 12, 1864, in English Papers, HEH.

35. London *Daily News,* September 27, 1864, quoted in Allan Nevins, *The Organized War to Victory* (New York, 1971), 141–42, Vol. IV of Nevins, *The War for the Union,* 4 vols.

36. Delos Van Deusen to Henrietta Van Deusen, August 21, 1864, in Van Deusen Papers, HEH; John Berry to Samuel L. M. Barlow, August 27, 1864, in Barlow Papers, *ibid.*

37. Nelson Chapin to his wife, January 4, 1864, in Chapin Papers, CWTI Collection, USAMHI; Simeon A. Garriott to Calvin Garriott, February 23, 1864, in John W. Royse Papers, PLDU.

38. John Hamer to Eveline Hamer, August 5, 1864, in Hamer Papers, HRT Collection, USAMHI; James Love to Molly Wilson, September 24,

1864, February 14, 1865, in Love Papers, Missouri Historical Society, St. Louis; Benjamin Stevens to his mother, September 8, 1864, in "The Civil War Letters of an Iowa Family," ed. Richard N. Ellis, *Annals of Iowa,* 3d Series, XXXIX (1969), 585.

39. Nathaniel Bright Emerson to his father, March 29, 1863, Emerson to his mother, October 19, 1863, both in Emerson Papers, HEH; Ephraim S. Holloway to John W. Holloway, August 7, 1864, in Holloway Papers.

CHAPTER 3

1. Roy P. Basler, ed., *The Collected Works of Abraham Lincoln* (9 vols.; New Brunswick, N.J., 1952–55), VIII, 332.

2. Dunbar Rowland, ed., *Jefferson Davis, Constitutionalist: His Letters, Papers, and Speeches* (10 vols.; Jackson, Miss., 1923), IV, 357; Augusta (Ga.) *Daily Constitutionalist,* March 30, 1861.

3. Thomas Pollock to his mother, November 20, 1860, in Abram D. Pollock Papers, SHC, UNC; William Nugent to Nellie Nugent, September 7, 1864, July 28, 1863, August 27, 1864, in *My Dear Nellie: The Civil War Letters of William L. Nugent to Eleanor Smith Nugent,* ed. William M. Cash and Lucy Somerville Howarth (Jackson, Miss., 1977), 132, 117, 129.

4. Elias Davis to Mrs. R. L. Latham, December 10, 1863, in Davis Papers, SHC, UNC; Edgeworth Bird to Sallie Bird, August 28, 1863, in *The Granite Farm Letters: The Civil War Correspondence of Edgeworth and Sallie Bird,* ed. John Rozier (Athens, Ga., 1988), 145.

5. Henry L. Stone to his father, February 13, 1863, in Stone Papers, Kentucky Historical Society, Frankfort; John Welsh to his mother and wife, January 26, 1863, in "A House Divided: The Civil War Letters of a Virginia Family," ed. W. G. Bean, *Virginia Magazine of History and Biography,* LIX (1951), 410.

6. Henry K. Burgwyn to his father, February 8, 1863, in Burgwyn Papers, SHC, UNC.

7. Edwart Porter Alexander to Bessie Alexander, July 26, 1863, in Alexander Papers, SHC, UNC; Eldred Simkins to Eliza Trescott, January 27, 1865, in Simkins Papers, HEH.

8. Paul A. McMichael to Margaret McMichael, February 19, 1862, in McMichael Papers, SHC, UNC.

9. "Robert A. Moore: The Diary of a Confederate Private," ed. James W. Silver, *Louisiana Historical Quarterly,* XXXIX (1956), entry of January 1, 1862, p. 306; Josiah Blair Patterson to William Bentley, Febru-

ary 26, 1864, in "Irrepressible Optimism of a Georgia Confederate in 1864: A Letter," *Georgia Historical Quarterly,* XXXVII (1953), 349; Louis Merz to his family, May 24, 1862, in *War Was the Place: A Centennial Collection of Confederate Soldier Letters,* Chattahoochee Valley Historical Society, Bulletin No. 5 (1961), 54; John Fain to his mother, March 10, 1865, in Archibald Henderson Papers, PLDU.

10. Phineas M. Savery to Amanda Savery, November 28, 1863, in Savery Papers, PLDU; John G. Barrett, ed., *Yankee Rebel: The Civil War Journal of Edmund DeWitt Patterson* (Chapel Hill, 1966), entry of March 20, 1862, p. 14.

11. Samuel Johnson, "Taxation No Tyranny," in *Samuel Johnson's Political Writings,* ed. Donald L. Greene (New Haven, 1977), 454.

12. Basler, ed., *Collected Works of Lincoln,* II, 250.

13. Charles Woodward Hutson to his mother, September 14, 1861, in Hutson Papers, SHC, UNC.

14. Lunsford Yandell, Jr., to Sally Yandell, April 22, 1861, Lunsford Yandell, Jr., to his father, April 22, 1861, both in Yandell Papers, Filson Club Historical Society, Louisville; James B. Griffin to Leila Griffin, February 26, May 21, 1862, in Griffin Papers (in private possession, cited courtesy of O. Vernon Burton); Edgeworth Bird to Sallie Bird, August 8, 1863, in *Granite Farm Letters,* ed. Rozier, 132—33.

15. John Lewis to his mother, July 31, 1863, June 10, 1864, in Lewis Family Papers, SHC, UNC; Richard Lewis to his mother, February 9, April 14, 1864, in *Camp Life of a Confederate Boy . . . Letters Written by Lieut. Richard Lewis* (Charleston, S.C., 1883), 82, 92.

16. Richard Henry Watkins to Mary Watkins, December 20, 1861, in Watkins Papers, VHS; Edward O. Guerrant to his father, February 15, 1865, in Guerrant Papers, Filson Club Historical Society, Louisville; John Thomas Jones to Edmund Walter Jones, January 20, 1861, in Edmund Jones Papers, SHC, UNC.

17. William Calder to his mother, June 26, 1863, in Calder Papers, SHC, UNC; John B. Evans to Molly Evans, June 28, 1863, in Evans Papers, PLDU.

18. George Hamill Diary, n.d. [probably March, 1862] (in private possession, cited courtesy of Pat Knobloch); Jonas Bradshaw to Nancy Bradshaw, April 29, 1862, in Bradshaw Papers, PLDU.

19. John G. Keyton to Mary Hilbert, November 30, 1861, in Keyton Papers, PLDU; Samuel Walsh to Louisa Proffitt, April 11, 1864, in Proffitt Papers, SHC, UNC; Chauncey Cooke to his parents, May 10, 1864, in "A

Badger Boy in Blue: The Letters of Chauncey H. Cooke," *Wisconsin Magazine of History,* V (1921), 67.

20. Thomas Key Diary, April 10, 1864, in *Two Soldiers: The Campaign Diaries of Thomas J. Key, C.S.A., and Robert J. Campbell, U.S.A.,* ed. Wirt Armistead Cate (Chapel Hill, 1938), 70; William Wakefield Garner to Henrietta Garner, January 2, 1864, in "Letters of an Arkansas Confederate Soldier," ed. D. D. McBrien, *Arkansas Historical Quarterly,* II (1943), 282; Allen D. Candler to his wife, July 7, 1864, in "Watch on the Chattahoochee: A Civil War Letter," ed. Elizabeth Hulsey Marshall, *Georgia Historical Quarterly,* XLIII (1959), 428.

21. William B. Bate to William H. T. Walker, January 19, 1864, in Civil War Collection, HEH. For an exhaustive discussion of this issue, with reprints of the relevant documents, see Robert F. Durden, *The Gray and the Black: The Confederate Debate on Emancipation* (Baton Rouge, 1972).

22. Jackson *Mississippian,* reprinted in Montgomery (Ala.) *Weekly Mail,* September 9, 1863, quoted in Durden, *The Gray and the Black,* 31—32.

23. Robert Patrick Diary, January 18, 1865, in *Reluctant Rebel: The Secret Diary of Robert Patrick, 1861–1865,* ed. Jay F. Taylor (Baton Rouge, 1959), 250; Richard W. Corbin to his father, December 29, 1864, in *Letters of a Confederate Officer to His Family in Europe, During the Last Year of the War of Secession* (Paris, n.d.), 89; James Branch O'Bryan to his sister, January 20, 1865, in Branch Papers, TSL.

24. James Wingard to Simon Wingard, January 4, 1865, in Wingard Papers, PLDU; Ethan Pennell Diary, April 8, 1865, in Pennell Papers, Missouri Historical Society, St. Louis; Joseph F. Maides to his mother, February 18, 1865, in Maides Papers, PLDU.

25. "The Diary of H. C. Medford, Confederate Soldier, 1864," ed. Rebecca W. Smith and Marion Mullins, *Southwestern Historical Quarterly,* XXXIV (1930), entry of April 8, 1864, p. 220.

26. Bell Irvin Wiley, *The Life of Billy Yank: The Common Soldier of the Union* (Indianapolis, 1952), 40.

27. Chauncey Cooke to Doe Cooke, January 6, 1863, in "A Badger Boy in Blue: The Letters of Chauncey H. Cooke," *Wisconsin Magazine of History,* IV (1920), 212; Walter Poor to George Fox, May 15, 1861, March 1, 1862, in "A Yankee Soldier in a New York Regiment," ed. James J. Heslin, *New York Historical Society Quarterly Bulletin,* L (1966), 115, 126—27.

28. John W. Ames to his mother, November 12, 1861, in Ames Papers, USAMHI; James E. Glazier to parents, January 16, 1863, in Glazier Pa-

pers, HEH; Edward H. Bassett to his family, December 1, 1861, in *From Bull Run to Bristow Station*, ed. M. H. Bassett (St. Paul, 1962), 12.

29. James H. Leonard to Mary Sheldon, August 15, 1861, in Leonard Papers, Wisconsin Historical Society, Madison; Uriah Parmelee to his mother, January 10, April 18, 1862, in Parmelee Papers, PLDU; Percival Drayton to Lydig Hoyt, July 15, 1861, in *Naval Letters from Captain Percival Drayton, 1861–65* (New York, 1906), 4.

30. Oliver W. Norton to "Cousin L.," January 28, 1862, in Oliver Willcox Norton, *Army Letters, 1861–1865* (Chicago, 1903), 43; Simeon McCord to Hanna McCord, March 11, December 15, 1863, in "Letters Home: Camp and Campaign Life of a Union Artilleryman," ed. Ruth K. Lynn, typescript in Box 1, Earl Hess Collection, USAMHI.

31. Franklin B. Howard to his brother and sister, March 29, 1862, in Howard Papers, Wisconsin Historical Society, Madison.

32. Charles Wills to his family, April 16, 1862, Wills to his brother, February 25, 1863, in *Army Life of an Illinois Soldier: Letters and Diary of the Late Charles Wills* (Washington, D.C., 1906), 83, 158; Henry Andrews to Susan Andrews, September 9, 1862, in Andrews Papers, ISHL.

33. George Lowe to Lizzie Lowe, August 17, 1862, in Lowe Papers, HEH; A. Fisk Gore to Katie Gore, August 5, 1862, in Gore Papers, Missouri Historical Society, St. Louis; Stephen Himoe to his wife, June 26, 1862, in "An Army Surgeon's Letters to His Wife," ed. Luther M. Kuhns, *Proceedings of the Mississippi Valley Historical Association*, VII (1914), 311–12; William P. Lyon to his wife, July 9, 1862, in *Reminiscences of the Civil War, Compiled from the War Correspondence of Col. Wm. P. Lyon*, ed. Adelia C. Lyon (San Jose, Cal., 1907), 50–51.

34. Charles E. Perkins to Haskell Whiting, August 3, 1862, in Perkins Papers, CWTI Collection, USAMHI; Lucius Hubbard to Mary Hubbard, September 8, 1862, in "Letters of a Union Officer: L. F. Hubbard and the Civil War," ed. N. B. Martin, *Minnesota History*, XXXV (1957), 314–15.

35. Arthur B. Carpenter to his parents, December 5, 1861, in Thomas R. Bright, "Yankees in Arms: The Civil War as a Personal Experience," *Civil War History*, XIX (1973), 202; Eugene Kingman to Charley Kingman, August 3, 1862, Eugene Kingman to Adda Kingman, April 7, 1863, both in *Trampling Out the Vintage, 1861–1864: The Civil War Diaries and Letters of Eugene Kingman*, ed. Helene C. Phelan (Almond, N.Y., 1983), 101, 158–59; Charles Wainright Diary, January 15, May 29, 1862, in *A Diary of Battle: The Personal Journals of Colonel Charles S. Wainwright, 1861–1865*, ed. Allan Nevins (New York, 1962), 9, 74.

36. Darius Starr Diary, February 4, 1863, in Starr Papers, PLDU; Thomas W. Stephens Diary, January 14, 1863, in Stephens Papers, USAMHI; George Breck to Ellen Breck, January 18, 1865, in "George Breck's Civil War Letters from the 'Reynolds Battery,'" *Rochester Historical Society Publications,* XXII (1944), 119–20.

37. Alexander Caldwell to his brother, January 11, 1863, in Caldwell Papers, CWTI Collection, USAMHI; Josiah Chaney to Melissa Chaney, September 24, 1862, in Chaney Papers, MNHS.

38. James Bell to Augusta Hallock, December 4, 1862, in Bell Papers, HEH; Constant Hanks to his mother, April 20, 1863, in Hanks Papers, PLDU.

39. Henry Henney to his family, n.d. [late December, 1862], in Henney Papers, CWTI Collection, USAMHI; Amory Allen to Elphany Allen, January 8, 1863, in "Civil War Letters of Amory K. Allen," *Indiana Magazine of History,* XXXI (1935), 361.

40. George H. Cadman to Esther Cadman, May 9, 1863, in Cadman Papers, SHC, UNC.

41. John Vliet to Mr. Bodge, February 2, 1863, in Thomas W. Sweeny Papers, HEH; John D. Shank to his father, February 17, 1863, in *One Flag, One Country, and Thirteen Greenbacks a Month: Letters from a Civil War Private,* ed. Edna J. Shank Hunter (San Diego, 1980), 59.

42. Simeon Royse to his father, February 14, 1863, in Royse Papers, PLDU; Olney Andrus to Mary Andrus, November 22, 1862, in *The Civil War Letters of Sergeant Olney Andrus,* ed. Fred A. Shannon (Urbana, Ill., 1947), 28–29.

43. "The Civil War Diary of C. F. Boyd, Fifteenth Iowa Infantry," ed. Mildred Throne, *Iowa Journal of History,* L (1952), entry of March 6, 1863, p. 375.

44. Chauncey B. Welton to "Dear ones at home," January 13, 1863, Welton to his mother, February 11, 1863, Welton to his uncle, March 20, 1863, Welton to his father, June 15, September 19, 1863, Welton to his parents, February 18, 1865, all in Welton Papers, SHC, UNC.

45. Marcus Spiegel to Caroline Spiegel, January 25, April 27, 1863, January 22, February 12, 1864, Spiegel, address to his regiment, February 22, 1863, all in *Your True Marcus: The Civil War Letters of a Jewish Colonel,* ed. Frank L. Byrne and Jean Powers Soman (Kent, Ohio, 1985), 226, 269, 315–16, 320, 244.

46. B. W. H. Pasron to A. A. Shafer, March 24, 1863, in CWTI Collection, USAMHI; James Connally to Mary Connally, May 18, November 5,

1863, in *Three Years in the Army of the Cumberland: The Letters and Diary of Major James A. Connally,* ed. Paul Angle (Bloomington, Ind., 1962), 58, 134.

47. William C. H. Reeder to his parents, December 23, 1863, in Reeder Papers, USAMHI; Benjamin Jones to Lemuel Jones, March 9, 1864, William Jones to Lemuel Jones, February 12, 1864, both in Miscellaneous Civil War Letters, Filson Club Historical Society, Louisville.

48. Robert Gooding to his brother, May 4, 1863, in Gooding Papers, State Historical Society of Missouri, Columbia; Phineas Hager to Sabra Hager, March 6, 1864, in Hager Papers, Clements Library, University of Michigan (typescript copy courtesy of David Holmquist).

49. Oliver Wendell Holmes, Jr., *Speeches* (Boston, 1913), 11.

INDEX

Alexander, E. Porter, 49

American Revolution of 1776: as inspiration for Confederate soldiers, 6–10, 50–51; for Union soldiers, 6–7, 27–30, 45

Black soldiers: as issue in Confederacy, 54–56; attitudes of Union soldiers toward, 66–67

Burgwyn, Henry, 49

Casualties: among Confederate soldiers, 17; among Union soldiers, 37

Class differences: in Confederate attitudes, 15–17; in Union attitudes, 35–37

Cleburne, Patrick, 54

Copperheads, 65

Davis, Jefferson: on Confederate war aims, 6–7; on slavery, 47; and black soldiers, 54

Defense of homeland: as motivation for Confederate soldiers, 18–21; for Union soldiers, 38–39

Drayton, Percival, 58

Drayton, Thomas, 58

Emancipation: and Union soldiers, 46, 54, 56–69; and Confederate soldiers, 48–49, 54–56. *See also* Slavery

Emancipation Proclamation: Confeder-

ate reaction to, 48–49; decision to issue, 60; and Union soldiers, 62–67

Foster, Stephen, 13

Fussell, Paul, 13

Grand Army of the Republic, 68

Grant, Ulysses S., 6, 63

Hammond, James, 41

Hemingway, Ernest, 12, 34

Holmes, Oliver Wendell, Jr., 43, 68–69

Ideology as motivation: among Civil War soldiers, 1–7, 68–69; in World War II, 3–4; among Confederate soldiers, 13–18, 24–25; among Union soldiers, 33–36, 41–46. *See also* Emancipation; Liberty; Patriotism; Republican government; Slavery

Jefferson, Thomas, 50

Johnson, Samuel, 50

Jones, John, 27, 30, 46

Lee, Robert E.: and black soldiers, 54; mentioned, 31, 38, 56

Liberty: as perceived war aim, 6–7; and Confederate soldiers, 9–11, 12–14, 25; and Union soldiers, 30–33, 34–35, 43–46; and relation

About the Author

James M. McPherson is George Henry Davis Professor of American History at Princeton University. His other books include *Battle Cry of Freedom: The Civil War Era*, winner of the Pulitzer Prize in 1989; *Ordeal by Fire: The Civil War and Reconstruction*; and *Abraham Lincoln and the Second American Revolution*. He lives in Princeton, New Jersey.